799.12    Merwin, John.
          Fly fishing.

$17.95

| DATE | | | |
|---|---|---|---|
| | | | |
| | | | |
| | | | |
| | | | |
| | | | |
| | | | |
| | | | |
| | | | |
| | | | |
| | | | |
| | | | |
| | | | |
| | | | |

# FLY FISHING

## A TRAILSIDE GUIDE
## BY
## JOHN MERWIN

*Illustrations by Ron Hildebrand*

## A TRAILSIDE SERIES GUIDE

W. W. NORTON & COMPANY

NEW YORK        LONDON

**Look for these other Trailside® Series Guides:**
*Bicycling: Touring and Mountain Bike Basics*
*Cross-Country Skiing: A Complete Guide*
*Hiking & Backpacking: A Complete Guide*
*Kayaking: Whitewater and Touring Basics*
*Winter Adventure: A Complete Guide to Winter Sports*

Trailside: Make Your Own Adventure is a registered trademark of New Media, Inc.

First Edition

The text of this book is composed in Bodoni Book with the display set in Triplex
Page composition by Tina Christensen
Color separations and prepress by Bergman Graphics, Incorporated
Manufacturing by South China Printing Co. Ltd.
Illustrations by Ron Hildebrand

Book design by Bill Harvey

Library of Congress Cataloging-in-Publication Data

Merwin, John, 1947—
Fly fishing: a trailside guide / by John Merwin;
illustrations by Ron Hildebrand
p.    cm. — (A Trailside series guide)
Includes bibliographical references and index.
1. Fly Fishing. I. Title. II. Series.
SH456.M476    1996      799.1'2—dc20      96-2141

ISBN 0-393-31476-6

W. W. Norton & Company, Inc., 500 Fifth Avenue, New York, N. Y. 10110
W. W. Norton & Company Ltd., 10 Coptic Street, London WC1A 1PU

1 2 3 4 5 6 7 8 9 0

*For Jason White Merwin,*

*With fisherman's luck,*

*And love from*

*Your Dad.*

## Books by John Merwin

*John Merwin's Fly-Tying Guide*
*The Saltwater Tacklebox*
*The Freshwater Tacklebox*
*Streamer-Fly Fishing*
*The Battenkill*
*The New American Trout Fishing*
*Fly Fishing: A Trailside Guide*

## Edited by John Merwin

*Stillwater Trout*
*McClane's Angling World*
(with A. J. McClane)
*The Compleat McClane*
(with A. J. McClane)
*The Compleat Lee Wulff*
(with Lee Wulff)
*The Compleat Schwiebert*
(with Ernest Schwiebert)
*Salmon on a Fly*
(with Lee Wulff)
*Well-Cast Lines*

## Contributing Author

*The American Fly Tyer's Handbook*
*Waters Swift and Still*
*McClane's Game Fish of North America*

# CONTENTS

# INTRODUCTION

These are the magic hours. Soft spring days when a warbler flashes yellow over a sunlit stream, chasing mayflies as they hatch from the water's surface. The trout, too, are moving; rising with gentle ripples to the insects in green shadows near the river's edge. The water is bracing, rushing cold around your booted waders, and the fly line unrolls in a long, graceful curve toward a patch of quiet water where the fly itself settles and slowly drifts. A dimple, then a tug. And then a trout, flashing golden sides like sunshine — a quivering bit of cold muscle in your hand; a darting disappearance when again released to the stream.

The deed is accomplished by an unusual mix of science, art, magic, and just plain luck that all together are called simply: fly fishing. It is for many people all-consuming, a way of life. For others, a sport to be taken casually as time permits. People fish for a variety of reasons, but my own favorite was described by the late John Voelker, an old friend who wrote under the pen name Robert Traver and was best known for his 1950s best-selling novel, *Anatomy of a Murder*. From his favorite trout haunt on Michigan's Upper Penninsula, Voelker once said that he fished, in part, "not because I regard fishing as being so terribly important but because I suspect that so many of the other concerns of men are equally unimportant and not nearly so much fun."

From its genteel beginnings along the brown-trout streams of southern England more than five centuries ago, fly fishing has gone global and now encompasses both fish and locations of every description. Fly fishermen now search Iowa farm ponds for bass and panfish as avidly as they search Montana rivers for trout. Nor is fly fishing strictly rural. Both New York Harbor and San Francisco Bay are hot spots for those seeking striped bass with fly tackle, and in the former case fish can even be reached by subway! Fly fishing is what you choose to make of it. Complex or relatively simple. Diverse or narrowly defined. And although its subtleties can seem daunting even to adult beginners, what's usually needed is someone to simply say: Use this. Stand here. Cast over there. And that's all there is to it.

That's the role of this book, an introduction for adult beginners that tells you all you need to know and no more than just that. You might look at these pages as your first date with an exciting, new sport. We'll get you through the mechanics of getting ready quickly, efficiently, and simply. Then we'll get to the romance. And that's where the fun is.

— *John Merwin*
November 1995

# WHY FLY FISHING?

Fly fishing is an inefficient method used for catching comparatively few fish. Its appeal is found in that paradox, one whose occasional rewards come with persistent, skilled labor and are valued all the more greatly as a result.

Mountaintops are probably of greater personal value to those who climb them on foot rather than arriving at the top by car or gondola. The lake's far shore is more satisfying when reached by canoe, but more quickly gained by motorboat. Some river rapids can be run by kayak or by megahorsepower jet sled, but the kayaker's intimacy with water is without peer. The bicyclist sees and hears more of his world at close range than a motorcyclist, although the Harley crowd will see many more miles. Each experience becomes most acute without mechanical contrivance or haste and is best derived with one's own two feet, a paddle, pedal — or a fly rod.

## MINIMALIST SPORT

Like the others I've mentioned, fly fishing is a minimalist sport. That does not mean simple, because it can become terribly complex if one chooses to make it so. Some fly fishermen will intensely debate such arcania as the gender of a prevalent

The trout — in this case a hefty rainbow — is the traditional quarry of fly anglers, but as the sport has grown in popularity, the types of fishes regularly taken on a fly has grown to include everything from catfish to striped bass to barracuda.

frames of exotic composites. Others just go for a quiet paddle, a walk, or a ride. Or simply go fishing.

There are many different kinds of fishing, of which fly fishing is just one. Each has its own devotees; each at its best requires considerable skill; and each has its snobs. There's nothing extraordinary about this. By comparison, some hikers may be disdainful of mountain bikers who in turn look down on those who whiz by on four-wheel all-terrain vehicles who are in turn sneering at those in big off-road trucks. It seems to be a scale of escalating technology with warring specialists on every rung of the ladder.

But you can be pure without being a purist. In the course of any given year, I do as many different kinds of fishing as possible; partly because I enjoy them all and partly because it's my job to write about them. But I don't put spincasting reels on my fly rods just as I don't take my four-wheel-drive truck down a "hikers

mayfly or the chemistry of nylon lines with the same enthusiasm that canoeists bring to arguments about degrees of hull rocker for Class IV rapids, that hikers bring to the boot-brand debate, and that bikers bring to oil-filled fork shocks and bicycle

66 Fly fishing is such great fun, I have often felt, that it really ought to be done in bed. 99

— Robert Traver (1974)

While the pursuit of fish with a fly may be viewed as the most refined and artful form of all fishing, the actual catch elicits the same simple elation and pride no matter what lure or bait was used.

only" trail. There's a place for everything, after all — except for snobbery, which I hope never creeps into your own fishing.

## A Definition

Fly fishing is just what it says — fishing with a bit of feathers and fluff contrived on a small hook to look like a fly or bug. This contrivance — "fly," henceforth — is essentially weightless, certainly far too light to be tossed some distance at which a fish might be caught. In other types of fishing that involve casting, a weighted lure is cast,

which pulls a thin fishing line along on its trajectory. In fly fishing, the bulky line itself is the weight, one that must be cast and unrolled gracefully in the air in delivering the fly to a distant fish. It is this act of casting a weightless fly that gives fly fishing both elegance and difficulty. There are many ways of fishing that are easier; there are none more lovely in appearance or feel.

The act of fly casting is more dependent on technique, timing, and style than it is on macho muscle. Partly for that reason, many women enjoy it as much as men do. Unfortunately, if one follows fishing in the *New York Times*, for example, one would readily conclude that the only women who fish are fly fishers. There are probably more women roaring around southern reservoirs in high-powered bass boats than there are fly-fishing through the Sunday *Times*, whose arbitration of style is no more than subjective. Again, it's not that one or the other is better; only that they're different.

If fly fishing is usually seen at the top of angling's caste system, then worm (or other natural bait) fishing is invariably at the bottom. In a way this is odd because both are simple, basic, and contemplative. As Louis Rubin points out in his perceptive little book, *The Even-Tempered Angler*, "For bottom fishing is no mere avocation, rationalization, or even technique. It is a distinctive way of looking at the world."

## A WINDOW ON NATURE

A fly fisher sets out to interact with nature as a whole, understanding that everything in the broad ecology of a river valley, bass pond, or saltwater marsh has some bearing on the fishing. Fishermen are thus birdwatchers, botanists, meteorologists, and more — all rolled into one. The presence of a particular plant will betray a streamside spring offering trout. The behavior of terns in the offshore wind hints at a school of saltwater fish. Wispy mare's tails high in the autumn sky predict a rain that will bring steelhead in from the rivermouth.

Perhaps no other sport involves so many and diverse natural dynamics. At the root of fly fishing's appeal is this fact: You engage the natural world in elemental form with a minimum of tools.

If all fishermen killed every fish they caught, there would be far fewer fish to catch — on some heavily fished waters, perhaps, none at all. Thus catch-and-release has become central to the fishes' and the sport's survival. Face trout upstream and gently cradle until they have recovered.

But perhaps too contemplative. Sitting on a riverbank waiting for a bite is like sitting in your kayak on the lawn: briefly pleasant and soon interminable. Almost — but not quite — pointless when activity is the point. The fishing, you'll find, is more important than the fish. At least most of the time.

66 In our family, there was no clear line between religion and fly fishing. 99

— Norman Maclean (1976)

## CATCH-AND-RELEASE

Sooner or later, you'll catch something and at that point will have to decide whether to keep the fish or let it go. Many people release most of their fish; some release all of them. Catch-and-release has become both ecologically and politically correct over the last few decades. This is not unique to fly fishing, of course; fish caught by virtually any method can often be released unharmed.

The ecological justification is very simple. If all fishermen killed everything they caught there would be far fewer fish to catch. So most of the time, I'm fishing for fun and release everything. But sometimes, if regulations permit, I keep a fish or two to eat. That's always seemed to me a commonsense approach.

Every sport has its extreme evangelists, I suppose. The ultimate in low-impact camping, for example, would be staying home, but that's not very reasonable. Some people take catch-and-release much further. Not only do they release all their fish — fine with me — but they're ready to loudly condemn my keeping anything as criminal. When confronted with this, you may explain, as I do, that you release alive almost everything you catch, but that fishing at its roots is a blood sport, whatever its modern veneer. I've already released a dozen today; the fish population is strong and healthy overall; so this one I'll eat this evening, thank you very much.

## STARTING OUT RIGHT

You need to know at the outset that fly fishing — and especially fly casting isn't easy. That's a radical thing to say, if only because it's contrary to the bushels of promotional material pumped out by fly-tackle manufacturers every year as they seek to draw new customers

Distance cast, striper fishing, Martha's Vineyard, Mass. Effortlessly casting big, heavy saltwater flies out toward striped bass takes the right tackle and plenty of experience. For all its simplicity, fly fishing is not always easy.

66 Often, I have been exhausted on trout streams, uncomfortable, wet, cold, briar-scarred, sunburned, mosquito-bitten, but never, with a fly rod in my hand, have I been in a place that was less than beautiful. 99

— Charles Kuralt (1990)

Most major makers and retailers of fly tackle offer one- to three-day courses of hands-on casting and fishing instruction. Taking lessons now means you'll have more fun later.

fishing is easily mastered.

The beginner, lulled into false confidence, unpacks and rigs his new tackle, ready for casting practice on the lawn. With his first attempt at casting, the line wraps around the rod and his neck and shoulders. The mess repeats itself over and over again as our poor beginner quickly concludes there's something personally and incurably wrong — an adult version of dropping the ball in your first Little League game. It's easy — so he's been told — so why can't he do it the same way he saw actor Brad Pitt casting in *A River Runs Through It*?

Here's a tip: Brad Pitt had a casting coach, several in fact, on the river-running set, and some of the really dramatic, swoopy casting scenes were done by professional fly casters as stand-ins. And what you need is a coach. People who accept golf or tennis or skiing lessons as part of learning those sports often don't realize that the same thing is necessary in fly fishing. Necessary, at least, if one wants the satisfaction of

into the sport. But those same makers do themselves and you a disservice when they claim fly

**?**

**DID YOU KNOW**

Fly fishing along with other types of fishing started to grow enormously after World War II as millions of returning soldiers not only went fishing but also started families who did likewise. According to surveys made by the U.S. Fish and Wildlife Service and the Census Bureau, there are now some 4.5 million fly fishers nationwide, a number that grows about 10 percent annually.

Fly fishing is usually associated with stream fishing for trout, but stillwater fishing shouldn't be over-looked. Sinking lines make fishing the depths more rewarding, and there is often action at the surface.

learning fairly quickly to play a good game without falling down.

This book will help, of course, both as an introduction to fly fishing and as a later reference. But the best way to start is with a fly-fishing school. Almost all major makers and retailers of fly tackle offer some kind of school, usually a two- or three-day

affair that centers around hands-on casting instruction. Specialty fly shops around the country offer similar coaching, often as one-day clinics where you can get your feet wet before committing yourself. Or you may be able to find a friend who's a competent fly caster and willing to get you started. There are

Even on remote Western rivers, it's important to keep stream etiquette in mind. Always respect fellow anglers, giving them the same solitude and quiet you seek.

also a variety of instructional videotapes available, which can help even though they can't tell *you* what you're doing wrong. There's nothing better than hands-on lessons from a pro, which can literally save you years of sometimes painful trial-and-error learning. Taking lessons now means you'll have more fun later.

Those lessons will probably be group lessons if you go to fly-fishing school, but your fishing afterward doesn't have to be. There's a noticeable tendency among novice fly anglers to flock or bunch up in small areas of popular fishing destinations. As if that's how it's done because that's how they learned. The sight of one fish-

Fish on! In this case a striped bass. Fly angling for saltwater species, particularly those found along the northeastern coast of North America, has become very popular in recent years.

## YOU CAN HELP

Trout, salmon, and other popular fishes depend on clean waters for their survival, and those same waters are constantly threatened by all sorts of environmental degradation ranging from chemical spills to logging clear-cuts to suburban sewage. Since it began in 1958, a national nonprofit group called Trout Unlimited (TU) has emerged as a powerful political force, an environmental lobbying group at both the national and state level If you fish, you need TU. For more information, write Trout Unlimited at 1500 Wilson Boulevard, Suite 310, Arlington, VA 22209; 703-284-9411.

erman seems to attract another, and so on until there are a dozen anglers spread the length of a roadside pool, 30 feet apart and chatting blithely about rods and fly patterns while making an occasional cast. There will also be a dozen or more miles of productive river that are empty of fishermen. Except for me, of course.

## MIND YOUR MANNERS

Manners and stream etiquette are ever more important these days as fishermen increase in number while the amount of available water stays the same. Here are three basic rules most beginners neglect, and that may eventually save you from personal embarrassment.

RULE 1: FIND YOUR OWN SPACE. Don't go splashing into a spot next to someone else. You'll scare the fish for one thing, while depriving your angling neighbor of the pleasant solitude he most likely seeks.

RULE 2: DON'T KISS AND TELL. If I show you a favorite spot, and you later show your friend, and he shows his friend...eventually there will be 20 people there. You won't like that. Neither will I, and I won't show you another.

RULE 3: DON'T BRAG. NOT EVER. Other anglers will occasionally ask if you've caught anything. If you have, the correct answer is "A few." Or "Nothing," as the case may be. If you say, "Wow, yeah! I got seventeen and the biggest was fifteen and seven-eighths inches," you will immediately be seen as a complete jerk who values the score over the experience.

### KEEP IN MIND

- Fly fishing can be simple or complex. It's your choice.
- Start right: Go to a fly-fishing school.
- Good fishing manners make everyone's sport more enjoyable.

# IN
# DUST
# WE TRUST

I had a long talk the other day with a young magazine editor in New York City about what's presently cool and un-cool in mass-media pop culture. Out here in the provinces, I told him, Pearl Jam is something you put on toast, and I'd never heard any of the other names of hot rock groups he was rattling off, either. In the midst of all this, the editor mentioned that he liked fly fishing. Why, I wondered out loud, does a new-media, twenty-something editor like to fly-fish for old-fashioned trout?

"It's because of the tradition," he told me. "There's a tradition there and a sense of continuity that's missing in pop culture, which changes every day. Fly fishing is like an anchor for me, even though I don't get to do it very often."

And so it is for many people. Fly fishing is a deeply traditional sport, perhaps more so than any other, and one that over several centuries has contributed to an incredible body of writing — more than 5,000 different fishing books in English alone, for example, extending back to the fifteenth century. Not only does this provide almost unlimited vicarious angling for rainy days and winter nights, it also offers a sense of belonging that one can obtain as easily as picking up a fly rod. Fly-fishing tradition, however abstract it might seem, is basic equipment — just like rods, reels, and flies — and is readily available to adult beginners.

You'll discover two things quickly in exploring that tradition and history. First, much of what's regarded as modern and new in fly fishing is not new at all. And second, much of the history you'll hear is only partly true.

## BRITISH BEGINNINGS

One good example of both is Dame Juliana Berners, said to be a British prioress who wrote *A Treatise of Fishing with an Angle* — a remarkably complete fishing text — sometime before the year 1450. There's considerable historical evidence that Berners never existed, and that the book was produced by a different — and still unknown — writer. But Berners's authorship has become fact by virtue of traditional acceptance, and her name often turns up these days as an early example of women in angling. The many anglers who regard catch-and-release fishing as a modern development, meanwhile, should note this advice from the *Treatise*, five centuries old:

You must not be too greedy in catching your said game[fish], as in taking too much at one time....That could easily be the occasion of destroying your own sport and other men's also.

Not all early fishing was fly fishing, of course. Izaak Walton's 1653 *The Compleat Angler* has gone through more than 400 separate editions as one of the most enduring titles in English literature, although its wide acclaim has everything to do with Walton's gentle, pastoral style and little to do with hard-core angling. Which is just as well because Walton was a bait fisherman who gave, for example, detailed instructions on fishing with live frogs.

Fly fishing didn't enter *The Compleat Angler* until added by Charles Cotton, Walton's much younger

Fly fishing was both celebrated and practiced nationwide by the early 1900s, when magazines such as *Forest and Stream* were offering equal parts of inspiration and information.

friend, with the book's 1676 fifth edition. Cotton was by most accounts an upper-middle-class layabout, seldom sober, who worked hard at rattling the seventeenth-century British establishment with reams of obscene poetry when he wasn't working out the foundations of modern fly fishing. His tackle was primitive by our standards: a line of plaited horsehair that he tied directly to the tip of a 15- to 18-foot rod because fly reels hadn't been invented yet. But his observations even now sound remarkably contemporary as he advised beginners, for example, that "to fish fine and far off is the first and principal rule for trout angling."

## EARLY AMERICAN FISHING

Fly-fishing for trout was well established throughout western Europe by the time large-scale North American immigration began in the eighteenth century. But while incoming Europeans doubtless brought their fishing

66 Angling may be said to be so like the mathematics that it can never be fully learnt. 99

— Izaak Walton (1653)

This assortment of fly-fishing artifacts spans more than two centuries, including notable American angler and statesman Daniel Webster (upper left) and trout enthusiast Bing Crosby (pipe, photo lower right). The earliest (1874) Orvis patent fly reel is at the upper right, while the fly rod at center belonged to author Ernest Hemingway.

gear, American sportfishing is little documented before about 1800, probably because it was one of the least remarkable things in an otherwise remarkable time. There are examples, of course. America's first fishing club was organized along Philadelphia's Schuylkill in 1732, while in Manhattan, Collect Pond was restricted to hook-and-line-fishing-only in 1734. But there were no American angling books or sporting periodicals before 1829, and many details of our early fishing history are speculative.

American angling's first literary light came with the 1847 publication of the first American edition of Walton's *Angler*, edited anonymously by George Washington Bethune. He was a short, fat, and often jovial (at least in print) Dutch Reformed minister, preaching in Philadelphia at the time his book was published under the name of "an American editor," apparently as Bethune feared a conflict between parish and trout pond. Bethune appended copious fishing notes to his Walton edition, which is still one of the most complete accounts of American angling as practiced before the Civil War.

The use of trout flies imitative of whatever the fish happen to be eating at a particular moment — that is, matching the hatch — is widely taken as a modern method. Bethune, however, dealt with that problem at length 150 years ago. Like many at the time, Bethune fished with two or more wet flies spaced on a single leader, and in coping with the trouts' finicky selectivity admitted to hedging his bets: "My practice is to observe the fly on the waters for my tail fly, and experiment with hackles on the drop [second fly on the same leader]."

**⁉️**

**DID YOU KNOW**
Many suppose eastern brook trout to have been the first trout encountered by early North American explorers, but that's not the case. Spaniards led by Coronado trekked through the Southwest in the 1540s, and narratives of that expedition include an encounter with "excellent trout" in northern New Mexico in 1541. Those trout were cutthroats — so named by angling author Charles Hallock in 1884 for the red-pigment slashes found along the fish's lower jaws — and that Spanish discovery is by far the earliest mention of trout in the New World.

## NEW FISHES

Bethune's trout were brook trout, which at the time were the only stream trout native to the East and upper Midwest. As America industrialized after the Civil War and as developing railroads combined with a growing middle class to foster widespread tourism, our brook trout were decimated by a combination of overfishing and pollution. This led to the American hatchery movement starting in the 1870s, a move that radically changed American fly fishing as trout hatcheries were

seen as a panacea for depleted waters.

Several millennia of natural, post-glacial evolution were altered

Prior to the invention of eyed hooks in the 1870s, wet flies were tied directly on short leaders called "snells." These are Civil War vintage snelled wet flies, which were then attached by their loops in series on a longer leader.

## A FLY-FISHING MUSEUM

Founded in 1968, the American Museum of Fly Fishing is located in Manchester, Vermont, near the historic Battenkill, long known as one of New England's prettiest trout rivers. The museum's collections feature extensive documentation on all phases of fly-fishing history, a large library, thousands of angling artifacts, plus tackle belonging to such famous Americans as Daniel Webster, Ernest Hemingway, Bing Crosby, and many more.

Exhibits are open to the public all year, and the museum also publishes an award-winning quarterly magazine devoted to angling history. For more information: The American Museum of Fly Fishing, P.O. Box 42, Manchester, VT 05254; 802-362-3300.

within a few decades as rainbow trout — native only to the West Coast — were widely introduced in the upper Midwest and East, while eastern brook trout were spread by rail and wagon as far west as California. And in 1883, brown trout arrived from Germany, soon becoming established in suitable habitat nationwide. Nor was the effort limited to trout. There were no largemouth bass in the New England states or far west until stockings were started in the 1870s, for example, and striped bass and American shad — both popular fly-rod fish — were introduced to the West Coast in the same interval.

There are two modern results from this ichthyological frenzy, one of which is that at least some of your fishing has become homogenized. You'll encounter two or three different trout species in a typical

---

## THE REAL THEODORE GORDON

His story has all the makings of a novel or movie: Reclusive genius with mysterious girlfriend dedicates life to fly fishing and literature, discovers major techniques while dying of tuberculosis. Legacy left in secret, ready for modern embellishment.

Theodore Gordon (1854-1915) is widely heralded by modern writers as "the father of American fly fishing" or "the father of dry-fly fishing in America." He was neither of those things, nor did he ever claim such. Fly fishing, including dry flies, was already being described in American angling books by Gordon's time. He was, however, a bright, inventive angler and fly tier who through widely published letters and articles early in the 1900s helped enormously to popularize fly fishing in general and dry-fly fishing in particular. Somehow from our compulsive need to pin down "firsts," Gordon was posthumously — and wrongly — crowned king. His reclusive personal life left plenty of room for later additions, a drafty cabin near the Neversink River in New York's Catskills added romance, and an old photograph of Gordon — a bachelor — fishing with a still-unidentified young woman added spice.

He was also more democratic than many of his later admirers, occasionally fishing for bass as well as trout. As Gordon wrote in 1912, "Once an angler, always a fisherman. If we cannot have the best, we will take the least, and fish for minnows if nothing better is to be had."

American stream these days, for example, where your forebears found only one or none. The other is that native species are often in trouble. In the Great Smoky Mountains, for example, native brook trout are now found only in ever-decreasing remote headwater areas because of competition with introduced rainbows. In the West, meanwhile, native strains of cutthroat trout — once the only trout in our Rocky Mountain states — are increasingly rare, partly from competition with a variety of introduced species and partly from inter-breeding with genetically dominant, introduced rainbows.

## EVOLUTION OF TACKLE

By the 1890s, increased numbers of Americans were fly-fishing for greater varieties of fish than ever before, all of which fueled some extraordinary changes in tackle. Fly rods before the 1870s were cumbersome and heavy, solid-wood affairs of ash or hickory and with flexible tips of imported lancewood. The development of split-bamboo rods — first produced in commercial quantities by Charles Murphy of Newark, New Jersey, in the late 1860s — was a phenomenon as these lighter, stiffer rods enabled fly casting as we now see it and helped to popularize dry-fly fishing after 1900. New tapered lines of braided silk offered a long, supple length of some weight that permitted casting for distance, and also by 1900 competitive casters were breaking the

## MEANINGS IN TIME

Many fly-fishing words and phrases have ancient origins that have little to do with their modern meanings. The word "cast" is one example. This once meant a fly-fishing leader with several flies attached at various points along its length; now it refers — in this country, at least — only to the act of casting.

Another example is the "X" designation used now to indicate sizes of nylon-monofilament leaders. A century ago, leaders were made of short sections of silkworm gut. Dried gut sections were drawn through diamond dies that shaved and reduced their diameters; 4X-drawn gut, for example, had been through four such drawings that ultimately determined its thickness. The higher the X-number, the finer the leader. The nomenclature remains long after the process is gone. Which is why your synthetic nylon leaders are 4X or other X-size of your choice.

magic 100-foot mark. The golden age of bamboo hit its peak in the 1950s with the work of makers such as Payne, Edwards, Gillum, and others — names that are now holy writ among modern collectors willing to pay several thousand dollars or more for prime rod examples that originally sold for a hundred or two.

The new and stunning technologies that came with World War II also brought the age of synthetics to fly fishing. By 1949, companies such as Fisher and Conolon in southern California were using new fiberglass-tubing technologies for fishing rods, and cheap, durable fiberglass quickly became the dominant rod material nationwide. Synthetic fly lines based on nylon with a vinyl coating came of age during the 1950s, quickly replacing braided silk.

Most important, clear nylon monofilament became widely available as a leader material after the 1940s. Previous leaders had been

made of silkworm gut; literally, the stretched and dried silk gland of a domesticated caterpillar grown fat on a diet of mulberry leaves. Gut leaders were stiff and brittle unless soaked in water; sections were short, so leaders contained numerous knots; and gut itself tended to rot and thus broke unpredictably. Nylon resolved most of these problems, and continuing advances in nylon chemistry are producing ever-decreasing diameters of extraordinary strength. As a

An exceptional example of bamboo-rod craftsmanship from the 1880s; in this case by John Krieder of Philadelphia.

result, fly fishermen are catching more and larger fish on smaller flies with finer leaders.

## THE NEW FLY RODS

Our now nearly universal graphite fly rods were first introduced in 1973 and have generally replaced fiberglass as the rod material of choice. Graphite is both lighter and stronger than either bamboo or fiberglass, which means the material bends and snaps back faster. When used in a fly rod of suitable design, graphite thus allows the fly line to be moved faster in the air. Most anglers are casting farther as a result, and with less effort than was possible just a few decades ago. In recent years, however, those same fishermen have been discovering that farther is not by definition better, which means many of the newest rods are being designed more for close-range precision than for distance.

Fly fishing has also gone global, thanks in part to jet aircraft but even more to computers. From my home in rural Vermont, for example, I get news of rising trout over the Internet even as the ripples are fading on a stream thousands of miles distant.

But while technology accelerates, tradition is paramount — at least in fly fishing. The fundamental equation of fussy trout and finely cast fly has remained unchanged for centuries. In a whirlwind world where pessimism often seems the rule, fly fishing remains as novelist John Buchan described it back in 1915: "the pursuit of what is elusive but attainable, a perpetual series of occasions for hope."

**KEEP IN MIND**
- Tradition is one of fly fishing's greatest values.
- Popular fishing history often isn't the real story.
- Many American fish like brown trout that are now taken for granted are, in fact, non-native, "exotic" species.

GEARING UP:

# RODS,
# REELS,
# AND LINES

F ly-fishing tackle is a system within which each component will be in balance and proportion to the others for best results. That will sound intimidating to some beginners, for whom there's a very simple answer. Almost all major makers and retailers of fly tackle now offer first-quality, entry-level outfits at a moderate price that include matched components — rod, reel, line, and often a leader and fly — ready for quick assembly and fishing. But whether you acquire your gear piece by thoughtful piece or go for a packaged outfit, you still have some basic choices to make and so that's where we'll start.

For openers, you'll need a fly rod, reel, backing, fly line, a leader, and a few flies. The overall cost here may range from well under $200 to as much as $1,200 or more, depending in part on your own budget, compulsions about fancy hardware, and how fast the salesman talks. But please, start in the moderate price range, remembering that even here virtually all available tackle far exceeds your ability to use it. A moderately priced outfit will last a lifetime with reasonable care and will also provide a sound foundation from which to expand later if you wish.

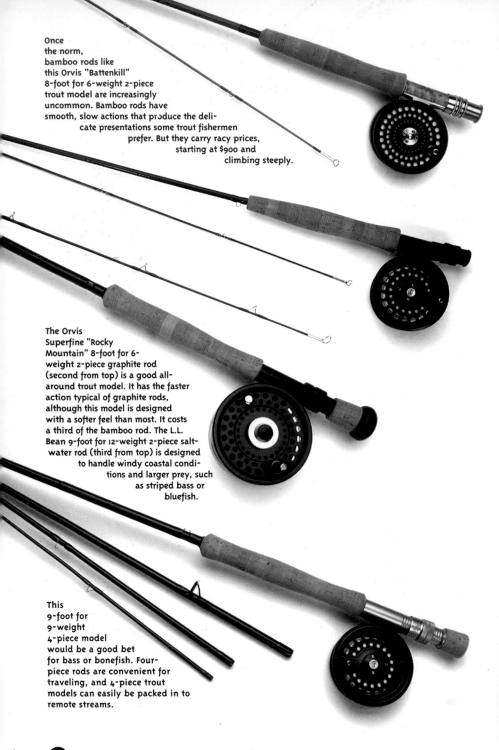

Once
the norm,
bamboo rods like
this Orvis "Battenkill"
8-foot for 6-weight 2-piece
trout model are increasingly
uncommon. Bamboo rods have
smooth, slow actions that produce the delicate presentations some trout fishermen
prefer. But they carry racy prices,
starting at $900 and
climbing steeply.

The Orvis
Superfine "Rocky
Mountain" 8-foot for 6-
weight 2-piece graphite rod
(second from top) is a good all-
around trout model. It has the faster
action typical of graphite rods,
although this model is designed
with a softer feel than most. It costs
a third of the bamboo rod. The L.L.
Bean 9-foot for 12-weight 2-piece saltwater rod (third from top) is designed
to handle windy coastal conditions and larger prey, such
as striped bass or
bluefish.

This
9-foot for
9-weight
4-piece model
would be a good bet
for bass or bonefish. Four-
piece rods are convenient for
traveling, and 4-piece trout
models can easily be packed in to
remote streams.

## FLY RODS

These come in assorted sizes; yours must fit both you and your fishing. Size is measured by length, commonly between 7 and 9 feet. Size is also measured by line weight; the common sizes are 1 through 12, with 12 being the heaviest. Both are usually indicated on the rod butt, right above the grip, such as "9' 5 wt." or "8' 3 wt." The best size for all beginning casters anywhere in this country is a 6-weight rod no shorter than 8 feet or longer than 9. Your rod should be of moderate action — not slow or fast. Most mail-order catalogs describe this distinc-

A complete outfit — including rod, reel, backing, fly line, leader, and even a handbook — can be a great way to start out. At a price of about $130, it's also an economical way to take your fist steps into the sport.

tion by rod model, or ask your salesperson. Men, women, and children who are about 5 feet 8 inches tall or less will be happiest

## GEAR TALK

### FLY ROD ACTION

The term "rod action" refers to the way in which a fly rod bends and unbends during the casting cycle. It's a very subjective term, and there are no industry standards. Not all rods are the same in that regard, nor is there any standard terminology. One maker's 5-weight, 9-footer might be stiffer overall than that by another maker, for example. Stiff rods require a fast, forceful stroke in casting, which is good for long distances, but their timing is hard to master. At the other extreme are very soft, slow-actioned rods, demanding of a slow and gentle stroke and designed for close-in precision — also difficult to use.

Your choice in rod action should be moderate. Not fast. Not slow. As a beginner, you won't yet have felt enough rods to judge the difference. Just make sure your salesperson understands that you want a rod of moderate or medium action, which is the easiest tool with which to begin learning.

with an 8-footer; taller people typically perform better with longer lengths up to 9 feet. That's a little arbitrary, but we need some definitions to get started.

Your rod will most likely be made of graphite. Alternatives are fiberglass, which graphite largely replaced as a rod material starting in 1973, and bamboo, the expensive, crème de la crème for fly-fishing traditionalists and also inherently difficult for beginners to handle properly.

Your graphite rod is a hollow, tapered tube with walls made of graphite fiber suspended in a hard-resin matrix. The fibers give the rod its stiffness or spring while the resin holds everything together. If you whack your rod hard against a sharp edge like a highway guardrail, the rod may break. Spring-closing screen doors, electric windows on cars, and car doors themselves also snap thousands of rods every year. Be just a little careful, and you'll be fine.

## WHICH ROD?

Designated fly-rod weights run from 1 (lightest) to 12 (heaviest). Light rods are for small flies, small waters, and small fish. Heavier rods take bigger flies and fish. Here's a basic chart for reference.

| ROD WEIGHT | FISH | WATER TYPE |
|---|---|---|
| 1 - 4 | Smaller trout, panfishes | Small streams; spring creeks; small, sheltered ponds |
| 5 - 7 | Larger trout, panfishes, bass, small saltwater fish | Larger rivers, ponds/lakes, protected (wind-free) saltwaters |
| 8 - 9 | Salmon, steelhead, bass, bonefish | Big rivers, lakes, saltwater flats |
| 10 - 12 | Striped bass, bluefish, big bass, tarpon | Any big, rough water or in any case where really large flies are used |

Most fly rods are two-piece, as your first one should be. Multipiece rods with shorter sections that stow more easily for air travel or backpacking are perfectly acceptable, but your initial two-piece version is easier to use. The sections are joined by a *ferrule*, a socketlike arrangement whereby one piece fits snugly into the other. There are various ferrule designs, but their function is obvious in all cases. Hold one section in each hand and put them together, making sure the little wire loops or line guides on the two sections are aligned as you press the sections firmly together. Now wiggle the rod a little while imagining a big trout or bass. Maybe even a salmon or steelhead. Good feeling!

Graphite rods are fragile when mistreated, but they withstand remarkable stresses when you need them most, such as when playing a feisty Atlantic bonito, like this one about to be landed off Martha's Vineyard.

Now take the rod apart. Grip the rod with a hand on each side of the ferrule and twist slightly while pulling the sections apart. If the ferrules are metal, as is common with bamboo rods, don't ever twist them, but use a straight pull only. Your rod probably came with a sack and hard, tubular case, and that's where your rod belongs when not in use. Uncased rods knocking around in the back of a station wagon are like putting the china shop into the bull pen. We'll start using your rod in Chapter 5, but meanwhile let's get the rest of your gear.

## FLY REELS

Here again there's a range of choices from complex, superheterodyne whizbangs that start at around $400 and run to thousands all the way down to more pedestrian, functional models that sell for less than $30. The best rule for beginners — and one that I still favor myself after 40

---

# GEAR TALK

## REEL DRAGS

Competition among fly-reel makers is intense, which means that many reels are overde- signed as features are con- stantly added in the war for new customers. For most freshwater fly fishing, you don't need a drag that "will stop a train," in the enthusiastic words of one maker. Presumably, you're not fishing for trains.

The classic click-pawl reel drag system.

Drags are assorted mechanical devices inside reels that restrain reel-spool rotation, thereby allowing restraint of a fish. The simplest — and best for most fishing — is a click-pawl system whereby a small triangular metal piece (the pawl) clicks against the teeth of an internal gear under adjustable spring ten- sion.

The most common mistake is in setting a drag of any type too tightly. Set yours so that the spool doesn't overrun and tangle when you give a sharp yank on the line. No tighter. Use supplemental restraint as needed by squeezing the line against the rod grip with your fingers or by pressing your fingers against the reel spool itself.

Saltwater fish are another matter, requiring not only additional backing capacity — to 200 yards or more — on larger, corrosion-resis- tant reels, but also stronger, more elaborate drags.

All fly reels look simple, but there is a surprising range in price and performance. A basic cast aluminum trout model (above right) with click-pawl drag costs as little as $35. The "TideMaster" saltwater reel (above and right) is carefully machine-tooled from bar stock aluminum. It sports an adjustable cork disc drag system and a price tag of $450.

brake, system will turn those dreams into nightmares by breaking your connection with the fish. The drag should be easily adjustable, especially at light settings. There are many kinds of drag systems, but for most fly fishing the best is a simple click-and-pawl.

years on the stream — is to keep it simple. Your reel needs:

ADEQUATE CAPACITY: That means able to accommodate your 6-weight fly line plus 100 yards of 20-pound-test backing line, about which more shortly.

A SMOOTH DRAG: Sooner or later you'll hook a big one that will rapidly pull line out beyond your dreams. A stuttering or otherwise erratic drag, or

66 If there is any one thing that a strong, hardy outdoorsman likes more than another, it is to catch a fish on some unusual makeshift tackle. Let a man use a ping-pong ball for a float and catch a fish that way and he becomes insufferable. 99

— John W. "Jack" Randolph (1956)

Their simplicity makes fly reels durable; they can last for decades.

along the rod grip, but the exact point isn't important.

Given those general parameters, a medium-size reel for your 6-weight outfit will be roughly 3.25 inches in diameter and single-action, meaning one spool revolution for one turn of the handle. Right-handers will cast with their right hand and reel with their left; make sure your reel accommodates a left-hand retrieve.

BALANCE: This is just a matter of proportion and comfort. A huge tarpon reel would be a weighty mistake on a light trout rod and vice versa. My assembled rod and reel have a balance point somewhere

## FLY LINE AND BACKING

In the interest of making things easy, fly-line makers agreed in 1963 to designate line sizes or weights by a simple number system. Before that time, chaos ruled and matching line to rod was very difficult. You want a WF-6-F fly line. Here's what that means.

The first two letters — WF — mean "weight forward," which is a line-taper design of greatest efficiency in casting. Others you may see

Plastic-coated fly line comes in an array of weights and specialized tapers. Some float, others sink, still others have fast-sinking tips, with the remainder of the line made to float. And they come in a rainbow of colors to help the angler keep them all straight. It is essential that the line weight match that of the rod.

include DT, which is double-tapered (read archaic), or L, which means level with no taper at all — an inexpensive but inefficient alternative. There are also specialty tapers for casting bass bugs and big, saltwater flies, and these lines are usually labeled by function. In all cases, the tapers (meaning a gradual thickness change at various points in the line itself) are designed for efficient energy transfer and accurate fly delivery as you unroll the line in the air while casting.

One hundred yards of 20-pound-test Dacron backing is your insurance against a truly big fish; an aggressive rainbow trout will go through 90 feet of fly line in less than 10 seconds.

The number is the line's designated weight, the precise meaning of which is irrelevant to most people. Just make sure the line number — 6 — matches the rod weight — in this case, also 6.

The last letter — F, in our case

## KITCHEN-SINK FLY LINES

Fly lines were made of braided silk until the early 1950s. Such lines tended to rot unless carefully dried, would float only if dressed periodically with a floatant, and were labor intensive to produce — meaning expensive. That all started to change in 1953 when upstate New York's Cortland Line Company produced a line with a plastic coating over a tapered, nylon core.

The big change came in 1960, however, when Leon P. Martuch patented a line in which a tapered coating of vinyl was applied over a level core. Martuch, who founded the company called Scientific Anglers, literally developed the process in his Michigan kitchen sink, dunking hanks of line in liquid plastic and heat-curing the results in the kitchen stove. A later process (1963) made the line float by adding microscopic hollow spheres to the liquid coating, and the modern fly line was born.

Playing a 10-pound striped bass on a June evening on Martha's Vineyard. When you're fishing for large, aggressive saltwater fish like stripers or bluefish, start with a heavy enough outfit: a 10-weight or heavier rod. Then make sure your tackle — reel, backing, line, leader, and fly — are in fighting trim.

## GEAR TALK

### FLY LINE CARE

The soft plastic surface of your line will eventually accumulate dirt and grit from both practicing and fishing. When the line seems to flow less smoothly through the rod guides, it needs cleaning. Unspool from the reel and wash the line in warm water and a mild detergent. Gently rub dry with a soft cloth. Do not use plastic-cleaning solvents, which will eventually cause cracks in the line.

— means "floating," a line for fishing on or very near the water's surface. You might also see an "I," which is intermediate or slow sinking; "S," which is full sinking; or "F/S," which means floating/sinking, in which case the forward part sinks while the rest of the line floats. These are specialty tools you'll encounter in later chapters. For now we'll start where most people start: with a WF-6-F on the water's surface.

Backing is just what it sounds like: extra help when things get critical. In this case it's extra, fine-diameter line behind your bulky fly line that keeps you connected to larger, long-running fish. Modern fly lines are generally 70 to 90 feet long, and a big, aggressive rainbow trout will pull out that much line in less than 10 seconds. A hundred yards of 20-pound-test braided Dacron backing is necessary insurance; not always needed, of course, but vital just in case. Never, by the way, use nylon monofilament for backing line. Nylon stretches, and that rubber-band effect multiplied by many revolutions of spooled line may compress and ultimately bend your reel's spool. Braided Dacron has negligible stretch and is used for that reason.

## LEADERS

Unlike backing, almost all fly-fishing leaders are nylon monofilament. Here the stretch is a helpful shock absorber between you and the fish.

Leaders also provide a tapered transition between the thick end of the fly line and a small-diameter connection to the fly. The taper is an important part of casting mechanics and smooth delivery. The leader's thick end is called the butt; the thin end is the tip or tippet. Most leaders are from 7 to 12 or more feet long.

Leaders are sorted according to X-size. The finest tippet is 8X, which is about 0.003 inch in diameter with a breaking strength of about 2 pounds. Sizes range up to 1X (0.010 inch/12-pound-test) and 0X (0.011 inch/15-pound-test). Stronger tippets are now referred to by their pound-test rating — for example, 20-pound — although older, now-archaic naming systems once prevailed.

The easiest leaders to use are knotless, tapered leaders that come in small packages labeled "7'-0X" or "9'-4X," for example. Length

66 The important thing in putting together an outfit is not to look for a line that will sail across the Missouri or a rod that will toss a lead sinker over the post office, but a modest set of tools designed to baffle a trout lying in plain sight. 99

— A. J. McClane (1965)

and tippet strength are thus shown on the label. Some fanatics, including me, will sometimes assemble numerous spools of nylon in different diameters for tying their own tapered leaders by joining different sections. You may also encounter braided leaders, which, however fashionable at the moment, are more expensive. I don't like them. They are deflected more easily by the wind; they don't handle large flies well; and tangles are more difficult to resolve than with solid-filament versions.

Remember: Keep it simple, and start with an off-the-shelf knotless taper. For the moment, we'll need a 9'-3X version for practicing with our 6-weight outfit. You'll meet other variations in later chapters on specific fish.

That's the core equipment you need for fly fishing. Take it out now and fool around with it if you want. Or you can wait while I get us through another chapter on a few more things you should know first. Then we can both go.

### KEEP IN MIND

- Start with a moderately priced outfit.
- 6-weight rods 8 to 9 feet long are best for beginners.
- Make sure your reel will hold 100 yards of backing plus fly line.
- Use off-the-shelf knotless, tapered leaders — solid, not braided.

GEARING UP:

# ACCESSORIES

Fishermen are notorious suckers for gadgets of every description — useful and otherwise. My own approach tends to be Spartan, mainly because I'm always losing or breaking things. Whatever the object, I try to decide if I really need it. If not, I can't lose it and won't waste time wondering where it is. There are, however, some things that I — and you — can't do without, so here's a rundown to which I've added a few price options.

## ESSENTIALS
### Fly-Fishing Vest
The uniform of trout, steelhead, and salmon fishermen worldwide since

Lee Wulff sewed the first one for himself back in the 1930s, the fly-fishing vest is a file system masquerading as a garment. (Most bass and saltwater fly fishers don't bother with these.) Pockets for everything will make your vest heavy, so make sure a support collar transfers at least some weight to your shoulders and not just your neck. Shorty-style vests are best for deep-wading anglers; these will extend down to about your lowermost rib. Make sure your fly boxes fit in the pockets, and look for construction quality. You'll get what you pay for in prices ranging from a serviceable $20 or so to nearly $200 for high-tech fishing fashion.

The fly vest is essential garb for the trout fisherman. This basic model sports 9 exterior and 8 interior pockets, 6 of which are special tippet spool pockets. The patch of lamb's wool on the left shoulder is for keeping frequently used fly patterns handy.

A large rear bellows pocket accommodates rainwear. The D-ring at the top is for attaching a landing net.

## Fly Boxes

Range from exorbitantly priced — but nice — British aluminum with multi-lidded compartments to utilitarian and cheap plastic. Make sure your flies will actually fit, which means compart-ments at least an inch deep

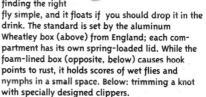

All those fly-vest pockets (opposite) hold fly boxes, compartmentalized containers in which to keep an assortment of fly patterns. A clear plastic box (left) makes finding the right fly simple, and it floats if you should drop it in the drink. The standard is set by the aluminum Wheatley box (above) from England; each compartment has its own spring-loaded lid. While the foam-lined box (opposite, below) causes hook points to rust, it holds scores of wet flies and nymphs in a small space. Below: trimming a knot with specially designed clippers.

for large dry flies. Newly popular foam liners will cause hook points to rust quickly if flies are stowed when wet. Loose, compartmented storage is simplest and best for drying. Clear boxes make finding flies easiest.

## Clippers

Essential for trimming knots. Buy nail clippers at the five-and-dime for less than a buck, or drop about $10 for the newest fly-fishing designs that also

## THE X-FACTOR

Many beginners have trouble matching fly size to the appropriate X-size of their leader. Too small an X-size for a particular fly means the leader is too flimsy to properly deliver the fly on the cast. Too heavy means the fish might spot your offering as a phony. Here's a simple formula for

making the right connection. Divide your fly size by 4 and use the resulting X-size leader tippet. A #12 Adams divided by 4 is 3; use a 3X leader. A big #4 streamer fly divided by 4 is 1; use a 1X leader. A minuscule #26 midge fly divided by 4 gives an equally minuscule 7X tippet. When in doubt, use one X-size smaller than indicated.

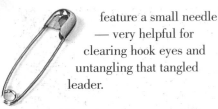

feature a small needle — very helpful for clearing hook eyes and untangling that tangled leader.

When you come up against your first clogged hook eye as a large trout is rising temptingly not 30 feet away, you'll sorely wish you had a safety pin. Some angler's clippers (right) come with hook-eye cleaners and other gadgets.

## Safety Pin

In case you bought the cheap clippers without an attached needle. Pin to the inside of your vest so you can find it when you eventually need it.

## Pin-on Reel

A small, spring-loaded gadget that will add years to your life by saving you time. Pin to the upper-left shoulder of your vest (right-handed caster) and attach clippers. Pull clippers down. Clip. Let go. They're retrieved by the reel, hanging ready for next time. Don't overdo it. A dozen hangy things all over your vest will tangle like crazy. Sign of the amateur.

## Fly Floatant

Any one of a number of water-proofing agents that keep your dry fly floating longer. Available as liquids, sprays, and pastes. I like pastes for ease of application and containers that don't leak.

## Tippet Spools

Small spools of monofilament available in the same X-sizes as full leaders. Trimming knots or breaking off fish will shorten your leader, in which case you'll be adding lengths of tippet taken from these spools as appropriate.

## TROUBLE SAVERS

● Keep your fly line away from solvents like insect repellent and gasoline, which will dissolve the finish.

● Nylon leaders are weakened by ultraviolet light exposure over time, an effect most pronounced on small diameters. Keep your tippet spools out of the sun, and buy fresh spools at the start of every season.

● Use dark-green or gray spray paint on clippers and other shiny objects worn on the outside of your vest, eliminating flashy reflections that scare fish.

## Sunblock

Those sunny days are dangerous; doubly so because you're taking a double hit. Direct sunlight plus intense reflections from the water's surface will burn you in a hurry. Skin cancer is in the news these days; hopefully, you won't be. Pay special attention to your face, neck, and backs of your hands.

Sun gloves protect hands from sunburn without your having to apply oily sunblock, which can make tying knots trying and damage fine monofilament tippets.

## Polarized Glasses

These protect your eyes from flying objects, such as that sharp hook that goes by your head every time you cast. They also cut surface glare, which means you'll see fish better in both fresh- and saltwater. Essential.

## Magnifying Glasses

Drugstore "grannies" for the over-40 set who need them for tying on small flies. Leave them home, and

Landing nets look great. More important, they help you land fish quickly, thereby allowing you to release them sooner and in a less exhausted state.

you can still watch the trout rising. But that's all you'll do.

## Insect Repellent

Carry it everywhere, always — even when saltwater fishing. Those aren't pelicans in the distance; they're salt-marsh mosquitoes. I keep my repellent bottle inside a small Ziploc bag as extra insurance against leaks.

## Landing Net

In many situations it will allow you to land fish

Forceps aid in releasing fish quickly by letting you remove small flies with ease.

bags avoid scaring fish near the net; shiny aluminum frames are trouble. Not essential, but a tasteful, wooden landing net also enhances the "classic angler" image; I always hang one on the ring at the back of my fly-fishing vest if there's a photographer around.

## Hat

Intensely personal choice of style. Good for sun protection, and a brim will enhance your vision. Baseball-style caps are the least vulnerable to blowing off in the wind, and therefore the most useful. I'm personally fond of old, battered Stetsons, but I also think the only thing worse than a new cowboy hat is a sign on my back that says "JERK." Now looking for a used-hat store to resolve this paradox.

## Forceps

Also called hemostats, these are slim, locking pliers useful for quickly removing small hooks from fish, pinching down barbs (required in some catch-and-release areas), and other tasks. Clip yours to the inside of your vest where they won't tangle.

Top: Two fly fishermen decked out for a day astream. The man on the right is wearing a shorty vest, his fishing partner a standard-length vest. He is also wearing a landing net shaped to make releasing fish simpler. Baseball-style caps like those above or felt-brimmed hats (below) protect your face from the sun and enhance your ability to see fish.

more quickly, thereby releasing them in better condition if that's your goal. Darker frames and net

The angler on the left will spend a drizzly day on the stream comfortably and productively, while the one on the right becomes increasingly sodden and sullen as rain dripping off her waterproof jacket saturates her cotton blue jeans. Aim for complete coverage or head inside to read a good book on the sport.

Saltwater anglers need sturdier, rust-resistant pliers with cutters for handling bigger hooks and toothy critters such as bluefish or barracuda.

### Hook Sharpener

The bigger the hook, the more important this accessory becomes. That means it's a saltwater and bass-

fishing must, but a trout-fishing option. I may be excommunicated for saying this as many trout-fishing perfectionists carefully hone the smallest of hooks. I don't bother.

### Rain Jacket

You don't need this unless it rains, of course. So if your predictions are

## GEAR TALK

### TIP YOUR HAT

When setting your rod butt and reel on the ground to string the rod, tip your hat first. Put your hat upside down on the ground, then set your reel/rod butt in the hat. That way you won't scratch a nice new reel. If it's a reel you've borrowed, this is even more important.

Breathable rainwear is by far the most comfortable, and worth its higher price. Buy a large enough jacket to fit over your bulky fly vest. A small clip-on flashlight (right) is a boon when you're changing flies at dusk.

perfect, leave it home. If not, it should live neatly folded in the large rear pocket of your fishing vest — ready at a moment's notice. The new (expensive) breathable parkas are by far the most comfortable. Make sure yours will fit over both a bulky fly vest and warm undergarment.

## Lead

Some sort of added weight on the leader may be desirable to get your fly a little deeper. The best kind of lead isn't. Nontoxic substitutes such as bismuth split-shot are becoming widely available, together with dense "putties," a fragment of which can be molded to your leader for getting deep. "So tell us, Mr. Merwin, about all those years you crimped lead split-shot with your teeth." Duh....

# GEAR TALK

### HOOK SIZES

Hook sizes are synonymous with fly sizes, meaning that a #12 Adams dry fly is tied on a size-12 hook. The larger the number, the smaller the hook or fly. The smallest is size 28 — about $1/8$ inch long — and the largest common fly hook (for saltwater use) is 4/0. Sizes range in even numbers only from 28 up to 2 (meaning there is no size 15, for example). After that is size 1, and as hooks continue to get bigger the nomenclature is 1/0, 2/0, and so on. Most common trout flies range in size from 16 up to 4. This system makes no sense. Its origins are archaic. That's just the way it is.

## Light

Small is beautiful; big will blind you. Necessary in late-evening fishing, but be careful. Your eyes will have acclimated to the dark over a long period, and if you can do whatever you need to do without using your light, that's a good idea. Otherwise, the glare will make you lose your night vision for as much as an hour. Your ideal light will be small and with a clip for attaching to jacket or vest pocket; there are many, widely cataloged styles. Excessive flashlight use will also spook some fish when you're fishing after dark — brown-trout and striped-bass fishermen take special note!

Look for waders with a built-in, zippered chest pocket, the ideal place to keep your car keys safe.

what's needed and you haven't anything else. Small, folding scissors will do; I use the ones in my ever-present Swiss Army knife.

## AND OTHER THINGS

Sooner or later, you'll fall in the water — everyone does at some point — which means anticipating a few contingencies. Ziploc-style plastic bags are useful in all kinds of ways. My billfold goes in such a bag before putting my waders on or getting in a

## Tape

Pull a foot or two from a roll of water-resistant, silver-gray duct tape; wad it into a small roll and keep it in a vest pocket. Use it to temporarily fix almost anything from leaky waders to a loose reelseat.

## Scissors

Most useful for on-the-spot alterations of flies — clipping the hackle from a dry fly, for example, to make it into a small nymph when that's

66 I'm not saying that all of fly fishing, yes, even baitcasting, is not a fine art...but I do think there are far too many people who are satisfied to accumulate tackle and terminology, rather than to fish. 99

— Negley Farson (1942)

surf or stream — I put my keys on a neck-lanyard clip under my shirt. That means they're not lost if I take a tumble, and that I can get at them easily even while wearing waders and other gear. A spare key also lives under my truck — sealed in plastic and securely bound with black-vinyl tape. I won't say where it is exactly, but you've got the idea.

Point-and-shoot cameras make capturing moments like this one on the Missouri River in Montana a cinch. Lightweight, smaller than a fly box, and in some instances even waterproof, they allow you to verify your fish stories.

Cameras are important, not only to record the catch of a lifetime before it's released, but also for when you walk around a riverbend and suddenly encounter the Methuselah of all moose. But if you don't carry a camera, you won't get the shot. I waded trout rivers for years with expensive photo gear around my neck, ready to loose serious bucks if I fell in and the cameras were

boat. So do a disposable butane lighter and a couple of candle stubs for emergency fire-building. And don't forget a change of clothes. There are dry trousers, heavy shirt, underwear, socks, and sneakers in an old duffelbag that lives behind the seat of my pickup truck just in case.

Your car keys deserve special thought. When fishing by wading —

When venturing farther afield, it's prudent to carry one of the ready-made, surprisingly compact first aid kits. A compass — accompanied by appropriate topographic maps — is another wise addition to your kit.

soaked. But no more. Modern 35-millimeter point-and-shoot cameras are superb, very compact, and often either waterproof or water-resistant. I bought one especially for a fishing-vest pocket and have had worry-free photos ever since.

In special situations, you may need special gear. I take a topographic map and compass on backcountry fishing trips, for example, and also take the compass when fishing the salt. Even when wading from shore along the northeastern coast, for example, the sudden onset of a fogbank makes all my visual bearings worthless. A compass has saved the day more than once, but only when I've checked bearings before starting to fish.

Some kind of first-aid kit is obvious forethought — maybe too obvious and thus often forgotten. Outdoor-oriented kits are widely available in various sizes by mail order, and of course you'll remember to carry special needs — prescription med-

icines, hearing-aid batteries, or spare contact lenses, to name a few. Some destinations may require special treatment. For a fishing trip to the Bolivian headwaters of the Amazon a few years back, I needed a number of preventive injections (typhus, hepatitis-B) that weren't available locally. Fortunately, my local physician had time to special-order them.

## Gear Bag

Bass and saltwater anglers are commonly fishing from small boats, in which case a gear bag replaces the trout-fisherman's vest. Multiple pockets in a small duffelbag help keep things in order, and yours should at least have a waterproof bottom to counteract water that invariably accumulates in the bottom of the boat. Your bag should also be large enough to accommodate both rain jacket and rain pants, as well as a warm jacket or sweater. Mornings and evenings can range from frigid along northern coasts to uncomfortably cool even near the equator.

Most equipment questions resolve themselves through experience and common sense. Which takes me to one final point. Many people who wouldn't dream of drinking and driving commonly mix boats and beer or head off to wade a treacherous rapid after a multi-wine lunch when a nap would be a better idea. While I've bent my share of tin cups at streamside, they're inevitably better bent *after* fishing.

When your quarry is bass or saltwater species fished from shore or from a boat, you may want to exchange your fly vest for a gear bag.

**KEEP IN MIND**

- Some gadgets are essential, but don't overdo it.
- Make sure your fly vest will fit *over* a warm jacket.
- Everybody forgets sunblock — at their peril!
- Worst thing to lose: car keys! Where are yours?

# FLY CASTING

A ll good things — trout as well as eternal salvation — come by grace and grace comes by art and art does not come easy." So wrote Norman Maclean in the widely popular book *A River Runs Through It*, and so it is with fly casting. Yes, it's poetry in motion, but you learn to write it one word at a time.

As you begin, make sure that your expectations are realistic. With an hour of practice, we can have you casting well enough to sometimes catch something — given cooperative fish — and without hitting yourself most of the time. But it will take years of con-

stant practice before you begin to match master casters like Mel Krieger, Lefty Kreh, or Joan Wulff, all of whom got there with time and thoughtful effort. Any tennis neophyte can lob a serve in his first few minutes, and thus enjoy the game; few expect to immediately serve up blazing aces like U.S. Open champion Pete Sampras. Fly casting is like that, however easy it appears at first glance.

Let's see how fly casting works in the first place. Remember that instead of just throwing a weight we're *unrolling* a weight — the fly line — in the air. The line unrolls in the shape of a loop, exactly like

Take care when putting your fly rod together and taking it apart. With graphite rods, hold the butt and tip pieces close to the ferrule and twist slightly as you pull them apart.

your feet. To fly-cast, you must learn to form and control a loop.

First, pick a good practice spot. An open lawn is okay — you'll need about 40 feet of open area behind and in front of you. The local gymnasium is fine, too. If you're the letter U tipped on its side. Casting loops can be narrow, almost V-shaped. This loop shape implies high line speed and distance; it's also the most efficient. Loops can also be wide — our U has a broad bottom — which means lower line speed and greater close-in accuracy and delicacy. Or loops can be nonexistent, in which case the line describes a large semi-circle in the air before collapsing in a whoops at practicing on an asphalt parking lot or other dirty, abrasive surface, be forewarned this will scratch, scrape, and cut the soft plastic surface of your fly line over time.

Assemble your rod and attach the reel to the reelseat below the grip. Tighten the reelseat band only enough so the reel is held without wobbling. Don't jam it down too tight; you'll need to take it off again later. If you haven't yet assembled

## TECHNIQUE TIP

### THREADING YOUR ROD

If you thread your rod by holding the slim end of the leader and putting it through the rod guides one at a time, the line will fall back through the guides if your fingers slip. Prevent this by doubling the end of the fly line, threading this loop through the guides instead. If you accidentally let go, the loop won't fall through the guides.

First attempts at casting are awkward and hark back to first steps on skis or first strokes in tennis or golf. But once you get the hang of its unique pull-and-push motion, it won't be long before you send dozens of feet of line zipping through the air. Note the straight wrist and perfect grip position of this angler.

the backing, line, and leader, do it now. Follow the instructions in Chapter 7 (on knots) as needed. You'll also need some sort of practice fly on the end of your leader.

Some use a short piece of wool yarn, or you can cut the hookpoint away from an old fly.

At the practice area, pull a dozen feet of line from the reel and

## GEAR TALK
### UNCOILING A NEW LEADER

Your knotless, tapered leaders are coiled within their packaging, the heavy end being wound several times around the coils to keep the leader from uncoiling in storage. Avoid tangles by placing the coiled leader over the spread fingers of one hand. Then carefully uncoil the leader starting with the thick or butt end, one coil at a time, until the entire leader is unwound. Straighten the leader by stretching it hard with your hands.

string the line and leader through the guides. The little metal loop an inch or two above the grip is a hookkeeper for storing your fly later; don't put your line through this. Then, with the rod butt and reel resting on the ground, pull about 25 feet of line (plus the leader) out through the top guide, letting the line accumulate in a loose pile on the ground. Then tie on your practice fly.

Pick up the rod by the grip with your right (casting) hand, making sure your own grip is correct (see the sidebar "Get a Grip"). With your left hand, grab and gently hold the line about 2 feet above the reel. Now — just for fun — cast. That's right; wave the rod around a little to see how it feels. Any old way.

While you probably didn't achieve a classic fly cast, you probably did notice that the fly line moved through the air and followed the path traced by the rod. You might also have noticed how hard it was to get the pile of loose line in front of you actually in the air and moving. What you've discovered is a major rule of fly casting: In almost all cases, a fly line can't be cast unless it's first straight. Straight on the water. Straight on the lawn. In the air. Anywhere.

Now set the rod down, pointing to the rear. (Make sure you or anyone nearby isn't about to step on it!) Then walk to the rear trailing the line in your hands so the line will lie straight back from the rod on the ground. Walk back to the rod. Pick it up by the grip, BUT keep the rod

## TECHNIQUE TIP
### GET A GRIP

Get a comfortable grip on your rod. Your thumb should be on top with your index and second fingers slightly extended. This is very similar to some grips taught in golf and tennis, and is also similar to the way in which your hand is extended when you're about to shake hands with someone. You may encounter some grip variations — index finger on top is one example — but none provides as good a combination of power and comfort.

## Fly Casting Practice

With about 25 feet of line extended to your rear on the lawn, pick up the rod and hold it with the palm of your grip hand turned up. Facing sideways, with the line and rod extended to your right (if you are right-handed) move the rod smartly forward (to your left) keeping it parallel to the ground. Let the line unfold onto the lawn to your left side. Do the same thing in reverse. You are casting.

tip down near the ground so the extended line is undisturbed. (See "Fly Casting Practice.")

Move your feet so you're facing sideways — the line and rod extended to your right. You're going to use your arm and wrist — palm up, side of the reel parallel to the ground — to move the rod smartly forward (that is, to your left) in a

■

## G E A R   T A L K

FROM CASTING TO FISHING

As your cast falls to the water, you're ready to fish — almost. Use your left hand to place the line under the index finger of your right (casting) hand. Then use that right index finger to squeeze the line against the grip. That way if a fish suddenly strikes, you're in control of the line and ready to respond.

For retrieving a cast with short strips of line — or for playing smaller fish — use your left hand to pull in line from behind your right index finger. Relax your right finger a little, strip with your left hand, then tighten up your right finger again. Repeat with each strip. This constant control will help in preventing missed strikes. Larger fish should be played directly from the reel to prevent tangles as a big fish may quickly pull out more line than you can control by hand.

Controlling the size of the loop described by your airborne fly line affects the presentation of the fly.

## Three Line Loops

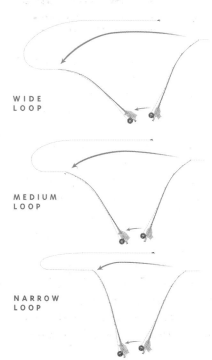

WIDE
LOOP

MEDIUM
LOOP

NARROW
LOOP

horizontal plane at waist level or a little above. Don't be too wimpy about this; fly casting does take *some* muscle, although not a great deal. Okay. Try it, remember not to move your feet, and hold the rod in position when you stop.

That was your first fly cast. The line has gone to your left side, is more or less straight on the ground, and the rod is pointing toward the left also. Now you can do the same thing in reverse, like a backstroke — a mirror image of what you did in the forward direction. And

The wider the arc of the rod tip as you cast, the wider the loop. A wide loop gives you low line speed for delicate, accurate casting. A medium loop takes care of most fishing conditions. A narrow loop gives you high line speed and the least air resistance for distance casting or sending flies into a headwind.

The forward push stroke as the wrist tips forward and just before the arm is fully extended. Notice how the rod tip is bent, on the verge of springing forward to release its energy and propel the line.

again. And again. Hopefully, you can see the U-shaped loop of the unrolling line. If not, try moving your hand and arm more abruptly through a shorter overall distance

66 The scientific and graceful art of throwing the artificial fly is a beautiful accomplishment, but not so difficult as is generally imagined. 99

— John Brown (1849)

in going from back to front. You may see the loop get more narrow as a result. Use a wider, longer stroke. Bigger loop, right? Lo and behold!

The reason I've started you casting sidearm (horizontally) instead of a conventional overhead (vertical) cast is because when casting in a horizontal plane it's easier to see everything that's going on. You don't have to look over your shoulder to check a rearward cast; it's right there in front of you. This makes it easy to experiment with different arm and hand motions and to watch what happens. Even after

40 years of casting, I still do this sometimes to get the feel of a new rod or to get my technique settled down when a rotten mood or a stubbed toe has blown my concentration.

Practice this straight-line, back-and-forth horizontal drill until you're able to straighten the line to the left and right in turn. More power. Less power. Longer stroke or shorter.

With rod tilted 45 degrees back, this angler is about to pause as the pull phase ends and the push phase begins. Her eyes appear fixed on the spot where a trout just rose on Spring Creek in Pennsylvania.

More wrist. Less wrist. What happens in each case will soon be evident as long as you practice thoughtfully. More important, you're starting to get the feel of fly casting. For which we need a little more theory, so let's take a break. Wind in most of the fly line, using your fingers to move the line back and forth right in front of the reel so the line spools evenly.

Now sit comfortably in a lawn chair. You can also do the following seated in your living room just by holding the butt portion of the rod and without assembling the whole thing. Grasp the rod grip with your right (casting) hand. Hold the rod so it points straight up in the air. While keeping the rod straight up,

## Casting Exercise

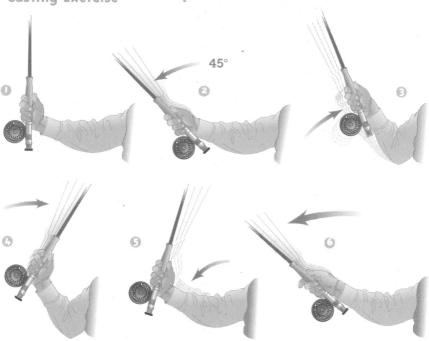

45°

1. Rod vertical, arm fully extended.
2. Tip wrist 45 degrees forward.
3. Maintain the forward tilt while bending your arm, retracting your rod hand toward your shoulder; the PULL phase.
4. Use your wrist to tip the rod slightly to the rear. Stop.
5. Keep the rearward tilt as you straighten and extend your arm slowly forward; the PUSH phase.
6. When your arm is almost fully extended, tip the rod 45 degrees to the front again. Stop. Do this a few times slowly. Then begin to blend the motions together.

retract or bend your arm at the elbow, bringing the rod back near your shoulder. Now straighten your arm, moving the upright rod forward until your arm is extended, rod still vertical. This back-and-forth, pistonlike motion is one-half of a good casting stroke.

Here's the other half. Read carefully, then do the following slowly (see "Casting Exercise,"). Rod vertical; arm fully extended in front of you. Now use your wrist to tip the rod 45 degrees forward. Move your wrist in one plane only; don't twist! Maintain the forward tip while bending your arm, retracting rod hand toward your shoulder. Now use your wrist to tip the rod slightly to the rear. Keep the rearward tip while straightening and extending your arm slowly forward. When your arm is almost fully extended — not before — tip the rod 45 degrees to the front again. Do this a few times slowly, re-reading to make sure you're doing it right.

The combination of pull-push arm motion and wrist tipping is the basic fly-casting stroke. The pull-push portion probably moves your hand back and forth about 18 inches or so; the wrist motion occupies only an inch or two. Now try slowly blending the motions together. Tip

Once you've gotten the hang of casting and false casting out in the open, it's time to hone your skills in the real world of streamside thickets and dense evergreens overhanging the banks, seemingly on all sides. It is safe to assume that more flies have been lost to plants than to fish.

forward, P-U-U-U-U-U-L-L. Stop. Tip back, P-U-U-U-U-S-H tip forward. Stop. Try it a little faster. Then go outside and repeat the horizontal exercise with what you've just learned.

For those who like a little theory, the extended push (or pull) motion of your arm straightens the line — remember how important that is! — and starts it moving. The wrist tip accelerates the airborne line and forms the unrolling loop.

Here are some common faults to keep in mind:

TOO MUCH WRIST: The most common fault. Remember that you're pushing and pulling the rod through the air, not flopping it back and forth with your wrist. It's not "all in the wrist"; it's all in the arm. Keep your wrist rigidly locked until it's time for the slight tip at the end of a stroke. And use a little muscle when you do tip, followed by an abrupt stop to transfer all that lovely energy through the rod into the unrolling line.

TOO MUCH MUSCLE: Women are easier to teach than men, as a rule, because women usually don't try to macho-muscle their way through learning to cast. Be firm, but not forceful. Harder is not better, while technique is everything. If things get out of control, take a break. Try again tomorrow. Remember this is supposed to be fun.

TOO MUCH TIP: Tipping the rod too much at either end of a casting stroke opens up the loop, making it wider. Try to consciously tip the rod a little less and watch your loops grow more narrow.

TOO LITTLE TIP: Not tipping the rod enough will often cause the line to collide with the end of the rod. Part of the reason why the rod is tipped in the first place is to get it out of the way of the forward- or rearward-moving line.

Now let's go back to the horizontal exercise. By now you'll have noticed that the line is almost straight to the rear and still in the air before it softly hits the ground. So keep it in the air, starting your forward stroke just as the line straightens in the rear and vice versa. Back and forth. Back and forth. Rest. Then try some more. Now you're fly casting; false casting, to be exact, which is the back-and-forth casting done before line, leader, and fly are delivered to the water.

As you practice false casting in a horizontal plane, try gradually raising the rod toward the vertical. You'll quickly see that the same false-casting strokes work at any angle; the hand and arm motions stay unchanged. Come gradually to the vertical, keeping exactly the same strokes, but now looking back over your right shoulder to watch your backcast. Hey, not only are you fly casting, all of a sudden you're versatile, too. Not bad at all.

To finish your cast — and start fishing — simply complete a forward stroke and let the line straighten and settle to the ground, following it down with your rod tip. Do not — never, never, never — add a little extra *umphh* to the last forward cast. However tempting, that common fault will only mess up what you've already practiced to near perfection.

At this point, you can cast about 25 feet of fly line. Adding a

> 66 It is just as well to remember that angling is only a recreation, not a profession. We usually find that men of the greatest experience are the most liberal and least dogmatic...it is often the man of limited experience who is most confident. 99
>
> — Theodore Gordon (1914)

Fishing on the North Umpqua River near Steamboat, Oregon. A classic high-speed long-distance cast with a tight loop of fly line speeding a tiny fly toward a hungry trout.

9-foot leader plus the length of your rod gives you 40 feet or a little more of total distance, which at least some of the time is enough to catch any of the fish mentioned in later chapters. If fish are rising or splashing farther away, walk, wade, or row closer — sneaking up until you're within your range. There are times, to be sure, when it's cast far or catch nothing. With the skills you've developed so far, you can learn long-line and other valuable techniques at a fly-fishing school or even from a videotape.

But now you've got the basic stroke. And you can control the size of your casting loop. Let's hit the water and see what we need to do to get around in the river.

### KEEP IN MIND

- Fly casting isn't all in the wrist; it's in your arm.
- The essence of fly casting is controlling your line loop.
- To be cast, your line must first be straight.
- Most fish are caught within 30 feet. Wading closer to a rising fish is always better than flubbing a long cast.

# W A D E R S
# A N D
# W A D I N G

Fishermen have been wedded to their rubber boots almost since the time of Walton. Early explorers found Amazon Indians wearing local-latex footwear early in the 1700s, for example, and by the early 1800s, Charles Macintosh in England had figured out how to coat fabrics with the new rubber material. Chest-high stockingfoot waders appeared as early as 1850, although waders with integral boot feet apparently weren't available until developed by upstate New York's Hodgman Rubber Company in the 1920s.

The wading itself hasn't really changed, either. Done correctly, it's the key to more and larger fish. But a mistake in judgment will get you wet, slightly hurt, or worse. Wading safety is equal parts common sense and skill. First and foremost, if you can't enter a particular wading situation confidently, don't do it. And if you can't swim, stay out of the water.

Consider also — when planning to wade to a particular spot — how you're going to get back. You can also anticipate the consequences of a possible tumble. Wading through rough water above a placid pool may not be a problem because eventually getting to shore will be easiest in calm water. But if the rough section occurs just above a still rougher canyon or rocky gorge, you might prudently forget wading.

When possible, keep your body sideways in the current to reduce water resistance. Shuffle your feet, making sure one foot is firmly planted before moving the other. Go around — not over — large rocks or other obstacles. In many cases, the long eddy behind a large rock will allow easy passage through otherwise fast water. If you do have to make a rough crossing, start upstream of your planned destination. Wading down and across with the current is much easier than wading across and up.

If you do fall in fast water, ride the current feet-first — protecting your head — until you can reach calmer water or can stand up. And no, your waders won't drag you down. While you're in the water yourself, water inside your waders is essentially weightless. While waders are cumbersome things in which to swim, swimming is possible, and the waders themselves won't cause you to sink.

Today the wide variety of available waders is simply astounding. Confusing, too, perhaps, until you realize they divide themselves into a few basic categories: bootfoot or stockingfoot; neoprene or lightweight styles.

## BOOTFOOT WADERS

These are chest waders with integral, molded boot feet, sometimes of rubber but these days more often of vinyl. Some boots may feature a fitted (tapered) ankle, which means it's less likely to pull free from your foot when stuck in the mud while also being slightly more difficult to put on in the first place. The bootfoot's big advantage over stockingfoot waders is in being easy to put on and take off. A disadvantage is that foot support is some-

Felt soles (top) are essential for most stream wading, where the rough felt texture cuts through slippery algae on rocks and thus grips. Cleat soles (bottom) are best for northeastern saltwater fishing, where you'll need traction on sandy beaches.

what less than
is obtained
with stocking-
foot styles
with which
you use sturdy
lace-up
wading shoes.
   Bootfoots
are widely
available with
either cleated
or felt soles.
Felt (or, com-
monly, woven
polypropy-
lene) soles are
absolutely
essential for
the rocky bot-
toms of trout,
steelhead, and
salmon rivers
where the
rough felt tex-
ture cuts
through the
microscopic
skin of algae
on many
rocks and
thus grips
well. Be

Fish on! It's when you're playing a spirited trout that you'll be especially thankful for sure-footed felt-soled waders. Between algae-covered cannon-ball-shaped rocks and water currents, getting around in the stream can make the most sober-sided angler appear tipsy.

warned, however, that felt is worse than useless on or in slick mud. Here there's no grip whatsoever, and your felt soles will turn into skis on slippery, muddy banks.

   Cleated soles, meaning a hard, molded tread pattern somewhat like a hiking boot, are best on mud or sand. Bootfoots with cleated soles are also best for cold, saltwater fly fishing as commonly done in the Northeast. The cleats work well on beaches, and more important, the molded feet don't pick up lots of sand. What little sand

that does adhere to the boots is easily knocked off before they're stowed. This is not the case with the alternative stockingfoot/wading shoe combination, which loads itself with sand to the point of near disaster.

Bootfoot styles are handy when I'm just going trout fishing for an hour or so and don't want to bother with more elaborate stockingfoots. Cleated bootfoots are great for wading small bass ponds, and I invariably use them in the surf. But they're a poor choice for long riverside hikes or on a day when I expect to be in waders for 8 to 10 hours or

more, in which cases I use stockingfooted styles.

## STOCKING-FOOT WADERS

This style of wader is just as it sounds: a waterproof, stockingstyle foot that requires both supplementary oversocks and special wading shoes. The addition of a sock between the wader foot and shoe minimizes abrasion — and eventual leaks — by preventing the wader foot from rubbing against the boot as you walk. Some wader makers claim this isn't necessary, but it is.

Modern wading shoes are superb. They can be laced tightly

Felt-soled wading boot. This model is made of a durable synthetic material that remains flexible after many wettings and dryings. Optional metal studs bite through mud and slime on rocks.

enough to provide adequate foot support, and are thick enough to prevent stone bruises on your feet while banging around a rocky riffle. Felt soles are typical. Many shoes are made of a synthetic

In a big, deep river a combination of stockingfoot waders and felt-soled boots are a must. And the warmth of neoprene waders is welcome when the water is lapping up around your ribs. Note the necessity of a shorty vest.

leather that stays supple through repeated soaking and drying, while my genuine leather wading brogues of years past used to dry to the consistency of steel.

Many stockingfoot styles feature an integral gravel cuff that folds down over the wading-shoe tops, designed to keep gravel and sand from entering. These are only partly successful. If tight enough to be completely effective, such cuffs would make waders almost impossible to slip over your feet. They are a handy place to tuck your laces, preventing tangles and trip-

## COLD KILLS

Early- and late-season trout and salmon fishermen are sometimes wading or boating when water temperatures are in the 40s. This water will kill you if you fall in and remain immersed for more than about 20 minutes. The insulating value of neoprene waders is critical here, and you might also consider a neoprene undergarment to protect your chest and arms. When trolling for landlocked salmon shortly after spring ice-out, I sometimes wear a light neoprene wet suit under my regular boating clothes — knowing that it may be the literal difference between life and death in the water.

Lightweight urethane-coated nylon stockingfoot waders are the answer in summer when neoprene is too hot but water temperatures are still too cold to permit wet wading. Notice how these anglers are holding their fly rods as they walk: by the grip but with the tips facing back to avoid snagging the tips and possibly breaking them.

## NEOPRENE WADERS

This is the same material used in the wet suits that scuba divers wear, a thin rubber-foam material whose advantages are warmth and stretch. In the case of waders, seams are typically sewn, taped, and sealed for waterproofness, making these effectively into "dry suits." Neoprene waders are available in both bootfoot and

ping. Cuffs are also available as an independent accessory for those waders built without them.

## TAILWATER TROUBLE

Tailwaters — meaning rivers below large dams — are popular trout-fishing destinations these days because their cold, controlled flow is very productive of trout. But in many cases, those dams are used for power generation, which means river flows may increase dramatically and without warning when the upstream generators are turned on. The shallow riffle you crossed in the morning may be an unwadable torrent by afternoon.

Before you wade a tailwater, check local sources to see if, when, and how much the water might rise. Many electric-utility companies provide such schedules, often through a special phone number. Ask at a local fly shop, hardware store — whatever you have to do to make sure. Once you do find out, don't forget to check your watch occasionally as you fish. If you don't, you'll be swimming — if you can.

stockingfoot styles.

The fundamental difference in neoprene choices is in material thickness, now more or less standardized at 3, 4, or 5 millimeters. Three-millimeter versions are the lightest and most comfortable, and offer moderate warmth. Fives are bulkier, a little less comfortable, and substantially warmer. I wear a 3-millimeter pair of stockingfoots for fall and spring river fishing, but switch to 5-millimeter bootfoots for December striped-bass fishing as well as steelhead fishing in midwinter.

It's worth noting that not only do neoprenes provide substantial warmth — even amid winter ice floes — but they also will remain warm even if a leak occurs. Such leaks happen less often these days as models continually improve, but when a leak occurs you're then wearing a wet suit and will stay comparatively warm even if damp. That's a substantial safety advantage when fishing in really cold water.

## LIGHTWEIGHT WADERS

Neoprenes are too hot for summer fishing in most areas. Fortunately,

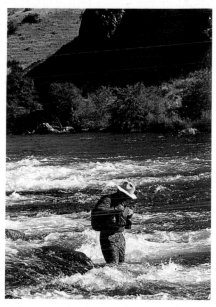

High summer, time for a soothingly cool wade, without any waders at all. Wading boots come in handy for this style of wading; never wade barefooted.

there are other, lighter-weight materials in both boot- and stockingfoot versions that will keep you comfortably dry while fitting loosely enough to allow some air circulation within the wader.

Options include lightweight, urethane-coated nylon as well as thin, stretchy rubber. In most cases, stock-

## GEAR TALK

### EXTREME CONDITIONS

When wading in really dangerous water — for example, fast and deep — even good swimmers might consider wearing a flotation vest. There are a variety of styles, usually tailored like a fly-fishing vest with plenty of pockets. These are bulky and uncomfortable, but they can save your life.

them in the typically frigid waters of a tail-water trout fishery even in August.

## THE ONE PAIR TO HAVE

If I had to chose one pair of all-purpose waders, they'd be 3-millimeter neoprene boot-foots with felt soles. In cold weather, I'd wear warm fleece trousers underneath. And in the summer, I'd fold the tops down to my waist, but still suffer. Happily I don't have to choose, which

Some fishermen still prefer hip waders, especially when they will be doing a good bit of fishing from the bank, where chest- and even waist-waders would be too warm.

ingfoot versions will fold compactly, which means they're great for traveling. Traditional rubber-coated fabric waders fall into this category also, but remember that none of the lightweights have any insulating value. They will be extremely uncomfortable at other than summer water temperatures, and I wouldn't wear

is partly why the disarray in my basement looks like a sportsman's landfill with waders hanging here, there, and everywhere.

### Wader Fit

Fit is a big problem, although better than it used to be. Some makers offer waders in short,

When the algae is especially slick and the rocks numerous and round, Korkers — carbide studded sandals — will give you the confidence of a go-anywhere tank.

reg-
ular, and
tall sizing, as
well as husky.
There are also numerous
versions cut for women. But
you'll often see a style you
like that is available only in
regular when you need a tall,
while your next choice might
be regular or tall when you
need a husky. Most mail-order
fishing catalogs have sizing
charts, which is a good start. But
for some people, the best answer
may be a pair custom-made to your
dimensions. Many of the better
mail-order houses offer this option
— especially in neoprenes — at a
premium price. If in doubt — and
especially if you're tall *and* large
— this is by far the best route.

The alternative is agony. I once
bought a pair of neoprene bootfoots sized to my foot as well as
"tall," according to my height.
For this particular manufacturer,
"tall" means beanpole, which I
am not. These waders fit my feet
and inseam, but the chest was
so constrictive that even
breathing was difficult. I
wound up slitting the sides
and cutting gussets out of an
old pair that I sewed and
sealed into the new ones.
This worked, but I still wish

# T E C H N I Q U E   T I P

## UNTANGLING YOUR WADING STAFF

Wading staffs are terrific aids that seem always to tangle somehow when
you stop to fish. I tie mine with a 3-foot-long piece of light nylon rope to a
D-ring on my fly vest. When I stop wading and start fishing, I put the staff
over my shoulder, where it hangs behind my back and partly in the water
instead of dragging in front where it would otherwise tangle my line.

I'd gone the custom route. In the long run, that would have been cheaper and easier.

## Other Needs

In some cases rock or ledge will be so covered with algae or otherwise slippery that even felt soles won't grab. The slick rocks of Connecticut's Housatonic River are one example. Oregon's famous North Umpqua is another. And there are some ledges along the Rhode Island coast, where I fish for stripers, that are roughly the equivalent of ski jumps. In such cases you'll want metal studs or cleats on your wader soles, offered as an option by some makers. Or you can go the sandal route; I use Korkers, which are lace-on carbide-studded sandals, the bottoms of which look a little like spiked golf shoes. Walking in these takes a little care and getting used to, but the net result turns me into a wader-clad, go-anywhere tank. The security is more than worth the trouble.

When buying waders, make sure they have integral suspenders or that a pair is otherwise included. If not, you'll need some. Wearing a belt is optional. Some people find it adds to the comfort of loose-fitting waders, but most neoprenes fit so snugly that a belt is superfluous.

Finally, consider a wading staff. There are a variety of commercial versions; an old ski pole with the basket removed will also work well. This is a third leg that helps substantially when you're trying to get around in rough, rocky water. I also use one sometimes in rough and rocky surf-fishing situations; it's just that much easier. Fasten the staff with a short rope to one of the D-shaped rings on your fishing vest and let the staff dangle in the current while fishing. When you're ready to move again, the staff is also.

### KEEP IN MIND

- Bootfoot waders are the most convenient.
- Don't use stockingfoot styles in sandy, ocean surf.
- Stockingfoot styles with wading shoes give the best foot support.
- Wade sideways in fast currents. Shuffle — don't lift — your feet.
- Felt soles are a must in rocky rivers.

# THE
# TROUBLE
# WITH
# KNOTS

Some years ago, I watched a so-called fly-fishing pro deliver a skills clinic at the local fly shop. When it came to knots, the guy was a whiz. He talked fast, almost urgently, and while talking tied a complex knot *onetwothreequick* — just like that. "If you can't tie that knot in 30 seconds," he told his audience, "you should be home practicing and not on the stream."

That made me angry. It still does. If I sit on a sun-warmed boulder surrounded by laughing water and take an hour to tie a knot, it's nobody's business but mine. I may miss a chance for a fish or two, but I'll relax in good humor while smiling at my own fumbling fingers. Eventually I'll get it. And you will too.

There's nothing mysterious about the various knots needed in fly fishing that a little practice won't resolve. It's a good winter activity; tie a few surgeon's knots in an old leader while watching the evening news, for example. In showing you how, we'll also try something new. Most published knot instructions involve diagrams of adjacent twisted strands floating in space. But how you manipulate your fingers — a pinch here, a pull there — is also important, and so we've added that to the diagrams.

That should help you overcome what many novices find to be a stumbling block.

Many of your knots will be tied with nylon monofilament. Remember to lubricate your knot with saliva before pulling it tight. That allows the knot to be cinched up tightly and also reduces heat buildup from friction in tightening, which weakens nylon. Monofilament knots break when they slip, so make sure yours are *tight*. Using pliers to pull on the tag (waste) end may help, and wrapping heavier lines around a wooden dowel will also allow stronger pulling while not cutting your hands. When you trim your knot, don't trim too closely as you may nick and weaken the line itself. And make sure you cut in the right place. More than once have I tied a knot only to absentmindedly cut the wrong strand, which left me no knot at all.

## ARBOR KNOT: BACKING LINE TO REEL

Pass one free end of the backing line around the reel spool above the line guard and back out again.

❶ Tie the backing line around itself with an overhand knot — also called a slip knot — and tighten.

❶

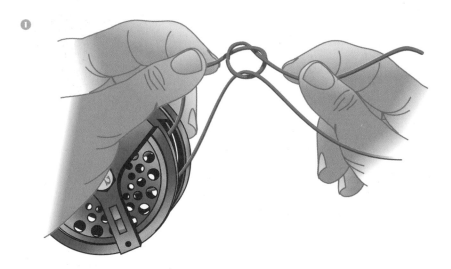

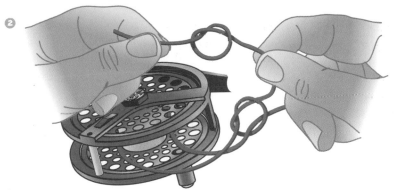

**②** Then tie a simple overhand knot in the line's end and trim. (This knot keeps the first from slipping.)

**③** Pulling on the backing line will force the knot back onto the reel spool. Keep pulling until the knotted end binds against the slip knot.

## GEAR TALK

### KNICKS OF TIME

Nicked or abraded nylon monofilament is seriously weakened. This line has a tough but microscopic "skin" that, once cut, allows the line's core to tear and break. Check your leader periodically by running it through your fingers under gentle pressure. You'll feel any nicks or rough spots even though you may not be able to see them. Cut away and replace these areas, or else risk losing your fish.

## ALBRIGHT KNOT: BACKING LINE TO FLY LINE

Now you've wound your backing on the reel, spooling it evenly. The end of the fly line sticking out of the manufacturer's packaging usually has a small tag reading "This end to reel." Pull 3 or 4 feet of backing line from the reel, an equivalent amount of fly line from the maker's plastic spool, and try this knot while seated with the reel in your lap. If you need reading glasses, now's the time!

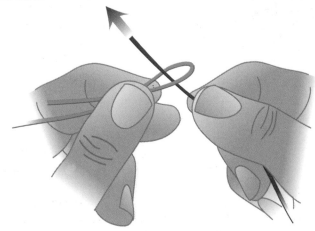

**❶** Double the fly line, making a loop about 3 inches long. Hold the loop with your left thumb and forefinger about an inch from the end of the loop. Grab the end of the backing with your right hand, pass that end through the loop from bottom to top, and bring the end up past your left thumb/forefinger by about 6 inches.

**❷** Then use your left thumb/forefinger to hold both backing and loop in the same position as in No. 1 above.

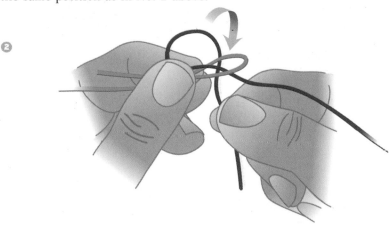

❸

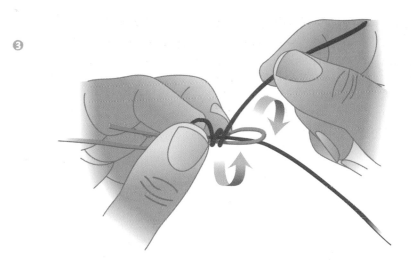

❸ Now use your right hand to make 6 wraps clockwise (away from you) around the fly-line loop working toward the loop's end. Each wrap should butt against but not overlap the previous wrap.

❹ Don't move your left thumb or forefinger. Do use the second finger of your left hand to press lightly against the wraps while making them to keep everything in place.

❹

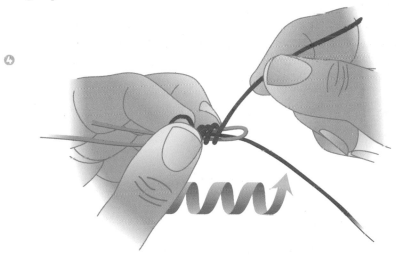

**5**

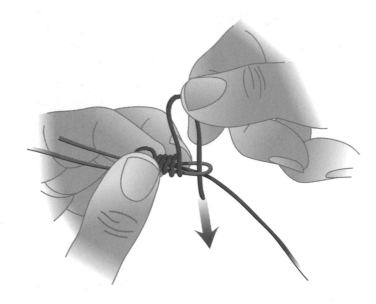

**5** After 6 wraps, pass the free end of the backing back down through the loop, top to bottom, so the line goes out of the loop the same way it went in. Your left thumb/forefinger haven't moved, and your left second finger still keeps light pressure.

**6** Now pull gently and evenly on both strands of backing beyond the loop to tighten everything *slightly*. Use your left thumb/forefinger to slide the wraps toward the end of the loop while you gently tug and tighten with your right hand.

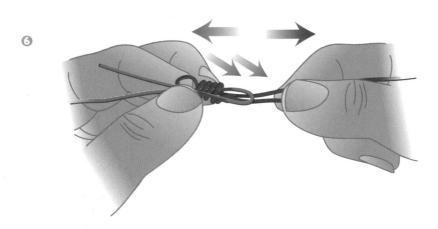

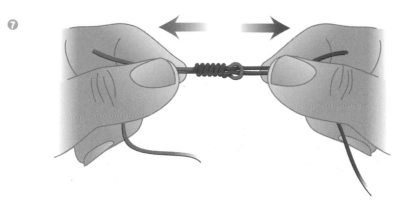

**7** When the wraps arc very close to the loop's end, it's time to tighten more firmly. Pull. Pull harder. Then trim the free ends closely.

## NAIL KNOT: LEADER BUTT TO FLY LINE

This seemingly complex knot goes quickly with a little practice. Sit comfortably in good light. You'll need a small-diameter, hollow, rigid tube. I use the tube on my fly-tying bobbin; some use a thin cocktail straw.

**1** Hold about 6 inches of the fly-line end in your left hand. The reel and rest of the line should be to your left. Hold about 6 inches of the leader butt in your right hand with the rest of the leader on your right. Overlap the two, grasping with your left thumb/index finger in the middle.
Place the tube parallel to and contacting the overlapped lines. Now your left thumb/index finger are holding all three together. As with the albright knot you'll be making wraps with your right hand while using gentle pressure from your left second finger to hold all in place as you go.

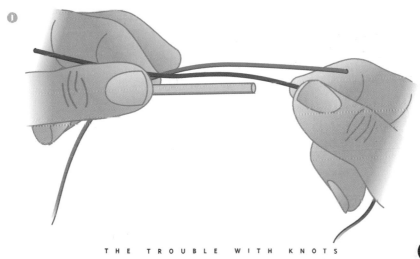

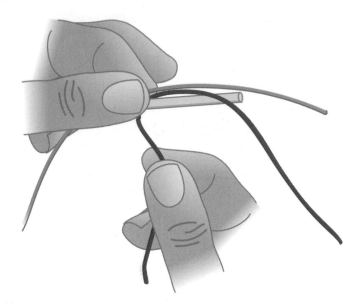

② Use your right hand to reach under your left to grab the leader butt.
③ Bring it straight down, then make a clockwise wrap around everything immediately in front of your left thumb/forefinger. The leader butt is stiff, which makes this a little tricky, but the rigidity of the tube should help as should pressing the wrap with your left second finger.

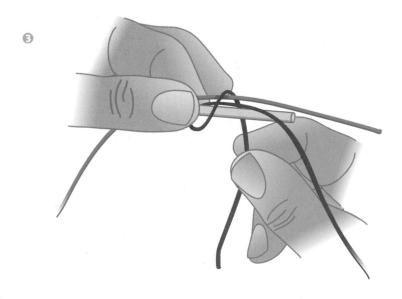

**4**

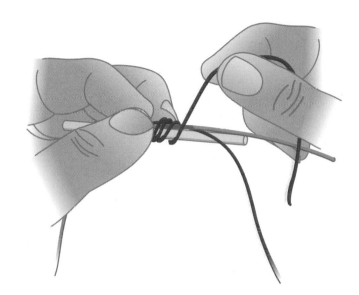

**4** Make 4 more wraps, each butting the previous one while not overlapping.
**5** Now use your right hand to slip the end of the leader butt into the right end of the tube. Slip it in as far as possible, which takes it through the tube and under the wraps you just made.

**5**

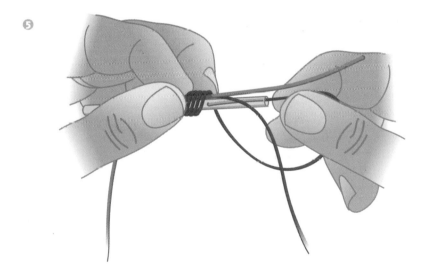

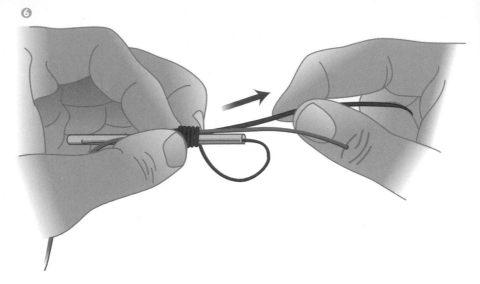

**⑥** Now gently tighten the leader from the right side with your right hand.
**⑦** While maintaining your left thumb/forefinger grip, reach behind your left hand with your right, grab the left end of the tube, and slip it away to the left, uncovering the leader butt.

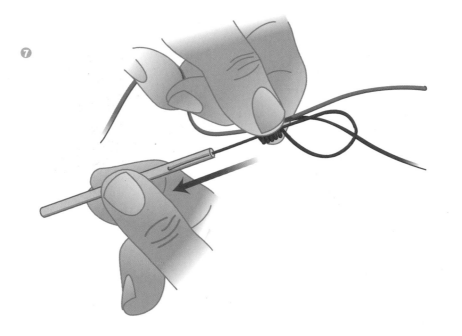

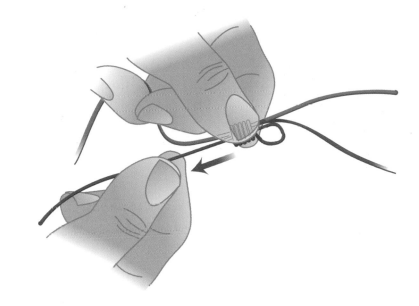

⑧ Then grab the leader butt with your right hand and gently pull it to the left.
⑨ Gently tighten the leader (from the right) and leader butt (from the left) again before relaxing your left thumb/forefinger grip.

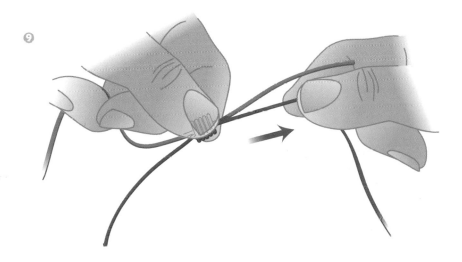

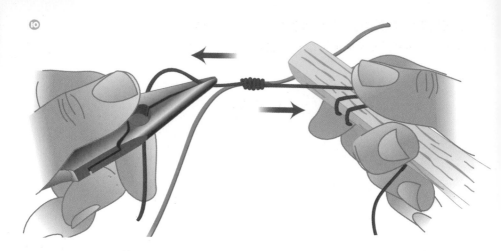

⑩ Now grasp the leader butt at left firmly with pliers and wrap the leader at right around a smooth piece of wood. Pull. Pull harder. Your partly tightened wraps are cinching down and digging into the fly line's coating.

⑪ Trim the excess leader butt at left and excess fly line at right. Test the knot by pulling on fly line and leader. Lightly coat this knot with a *small amount* of flexible cement such as PlioBond or ShoeGoo so the knot will slide through the rod guides more easily.

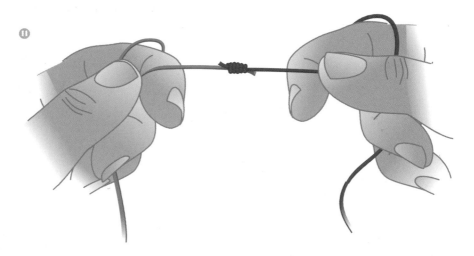

# SURGEON'S KNOT: TIPPET TO LEADER

A very simple knot as long as you pinch in the right place.

**❶**

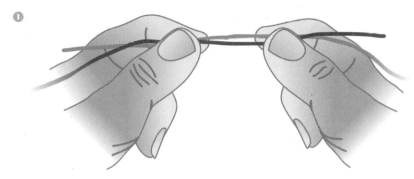

❶ Overlap leader end and end of tippet section by about 6 inches. Grasp both sections with right thumb and index finger in middle of overlap. Use your left hand to slide the assembly to the left so only about 2 inches of tippet section remains to the right of your right thumb/index finger grip.

❷ With your left palm facing up and underneath the overlapped lines, grasp the two with left thumb/index finger about 2 inches to the left of your right thumb. Rotate your left hand toward your body while moving your left hand toward your right thumb. This will form a loop in the doubled lines between your hands. Use your right thumb/index finger to pinch the intersection at the bottom of the loop, now effectively pinching 4 strands.

**❷**

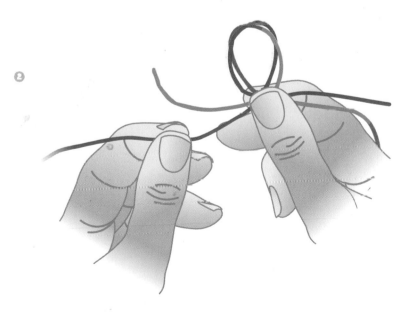

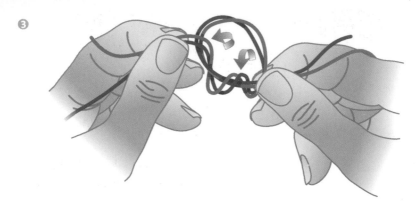

❸ Use your right hand to pass both tippet section and leader end though the loop from back to front. In shape, this is a simple overhand knot, but don't tighten yet. Pinch the intersection with left thumb/index finger. Pass leader and tippet section through the loop again with your right hand — a double overhand knot.

❹ Grasp the leader ends and tippet section end on left and right sides of the knot with left and right hands and tighten gently and evenly.

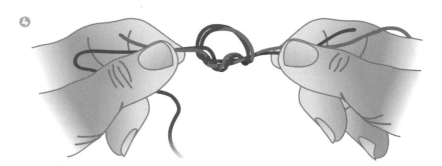

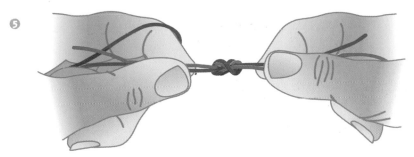

**⑤** Repeat: evenly. Uneven tightening seriously weakens this knot. If things seem awry as you start to tighten, stop and pull gently on a single strand until things are even again.

**⑥** Trim excess ends.

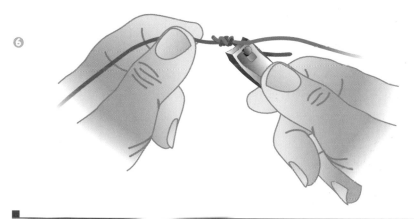

## WIND KNOTS

Sometimes you'll discover that a small, tight overhand knot has mysteriously appeared in your leader, usually in the tippet area near the fly. Fly fishers traditionally call these "wind knots," but they have nothing to do with the wind. They are caused by sloppy casting, in which case the line, leader, and fly collide in the air, sometimes knotting themselves.

Wind knots weaken line strength by more than 50 percent. It's often tempting to say the heck with it, and to just leave the knot in the leader while continuing to fish. Small fish probably won't cause this knot to break; big fish will break it. Want to catch larger fish? Cut away the wind knot and re-tie your fly!

## DOUBLE TURLE KNOT: LEADER TO FLY

There are many different terminal knots, meaning leader to fly. This is the easiest, and I use it for everything from steelhead and salmon flies on heavy leaders down to tiny midges fished on fragile 8X. This knot must be used on flies with hook eyes that are turned either up or down, which are the most common styles.

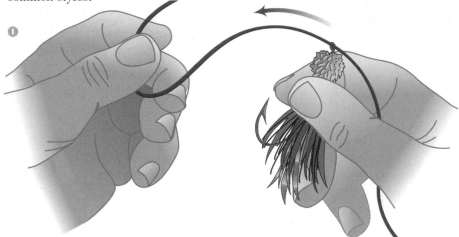

**❶** Thread leader tippet through hook eye so the free end extends a foot or more beyond the fly. Grasp the free end beyond the fly, letting the fly slide on down the leader. The object is to tie a 2-turn slipping loop.

**❷** Grasp the leader about a foot from the end with the last three fingers of your right hand, keeping thumb and index finger free. Use your left hand to pass the leader under itself near your right hand, forming a large loop with a few inches of tippet extending beyond the intersection. Pinch the intersection with your right thumb/index finger.

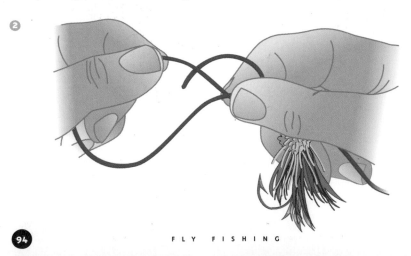

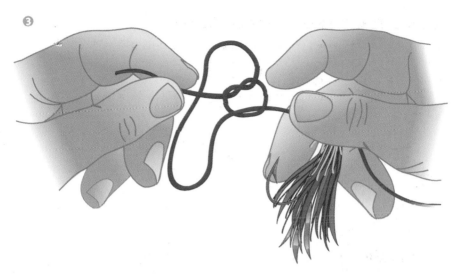

**❸** Tip the intersection and tippet free end upward by rotating your right hand clockwise (away from you), then tie a double-overhand knot with left and right hands.

**❹** Remember to keep an open leader loop to your left.

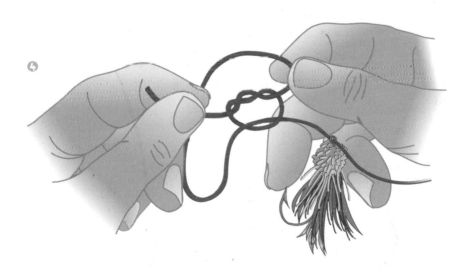

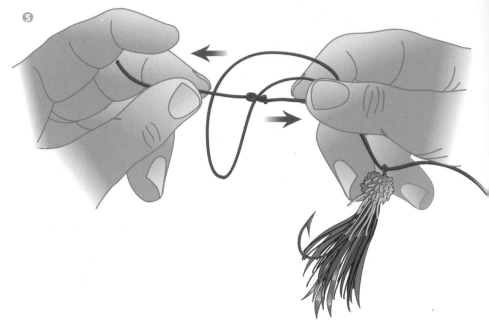

**5** Tighten the knot gently — not fully tight yet.
**6** Slide the fly back up the leader and pass the fly through the loop from bottom to top.

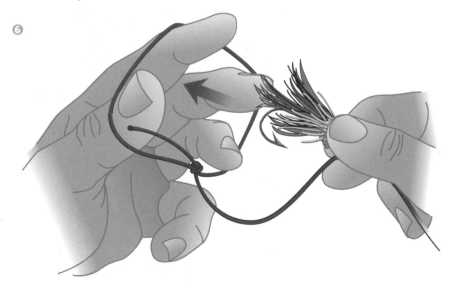

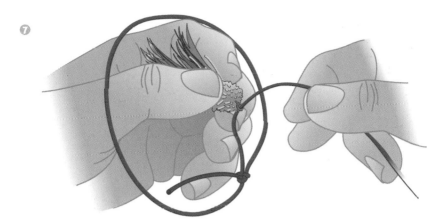

**7** Grasp the fly with your left thumb/index finger near — but not covering — the fly's head.

**8** Gently and gradually pull on the leader with your right hand. The loop will slip, gradually become smaller, and start to tighten near the fly's head.

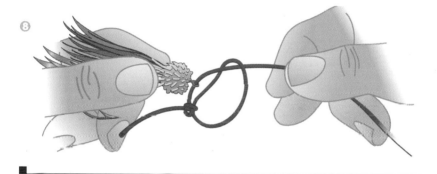

## MORE KNOTS

While I've shown you enough knots to get you started, eventually you'll need to learn more. There are special knots for attaching wire leader tippets, for example, and still more for use with special kinds of hooks.

The easy answer is the excel-lent *Practical Fishing Knots — II* by Lefty Kreh and Mark Sosin. This $10 paperback shows you all you need to know and more. The diagrams are excellent. Can be obtained from bookstores, fly-fishing shops, or the publisher, Lyons and Burford Publishers, 31 West 21st Street, New York, NY 10010.

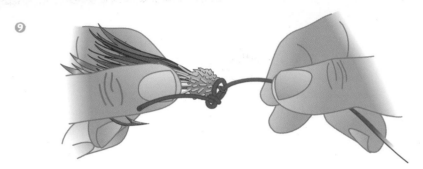

**⑨** When the loop has become quite small but not yet tight, make sure it seats immediately behind the hook eye, effectively wrapped around the thread or varnish that makes up the head of the fly.

**⑩** Now tighten fully and trim. When attaching tiny flies to ultra-fine tippets with various knots, many people wind up with an aggravating curlicue in the monofilament immediately in front of the fly. Trout don't like this, either. This happens when fine nylon is pulled around the hook eye under tension, much like curling a Christmas ribbon with the edge of your scissors. You can avoid this problem by not fully tightening your Turle knot until it's very nearly seated. Gently get it almost there, and only then tighten. Your friends will ask you how you did it.

### KEEP IN MIND

- Most knots break because they slip. Make yours tight!
- Lubricate your knots with saliva while tightening.
- Finger pressure here and there is just as critical as what strand goes where. Practice *both*.
- Prolonged exposure to sunlight weakens nylon monofilament. Use fresh material.

# FLY
# FISHING
# FOR
# TROUT

The jewel-like brook trout sculling through spruce shadows in a New Hampshire pond are a far cry from the brown trout smashing stoneflies in the torrents of Montana's Madison River. And the rising rainbows of northern California's Fall River seem a very different fish from a Colorado cutthroat trout. These are America's trout: four widely spread species as diverse geographically as they appear close-up. But they're all trout that behave in similar ways, which happily allows fly-fishing tactics to be essentially similar from Alaska to Maine and everywhere in between.

## THE EDGE CONCEPT

Stream fishing for trout generally means fishing the edges, an idea that not only defines where and how you fish, but also relates to the innate behavioral patterns of the fish themselves. An edge is nothing more or less than it sounds: the edge where a streamside log meets the water, the edge of a midstream boulder, the intersection or edge of fast and slow currents, or the bankside edge of the stream itself. Trout favor these edges because such spots typically offer some combination of food and shelter.

While rising trout are at times found in other areas of a stream — randomly rising over the length of a broad pool, as one example — edges are as close to being a rule as one finds in trout fishing. A trout holding in slow water adjacent to a fast current has easy water in which to swim, thereby conserving energy. At the same time, the trout can pluck food from the nearby fast water that brings insects and other drifting fare in greatest abundance. As another example, a trout may feed near a streambank stump, obtaining ample food while ready to dart under the nearby cover if an otter, fisherman, or other predator happens along. It is this fragile balance between survival and efficient feeding that most often determines where trout are found, and much of the time that means edges.

## Ponds and Lakes

Edges are important in trout-pond fishing, too, but for different reasons. In stream fishing, the water moves and fish feed while often remaining in a single spot, taking what's brought to them by the current. In ponds and lakes, the water isn't moving — hence the name "stillwater" trout fishing — so the trout have to swim around to find food.

In the latter case, edges relate to food sources. Underwater weedbeds, for example, typically hold more and different insect forms than does an open underwater plain. This means the edge of a weedbed is a likely spot to cast your slow-sinking line with a small Hare's Ear or other nymph attached, hoping to intercept a cruising trout. If that weedbed edge comes at the juncture of deep and shallow water, so much the better — kind of a double edge that can be even more productive. Underwater rock piles, points, gravel- or sandbars, and a lake's inlet and outlet channels are other important edge examples in pond and lake fishing for trout.

## UNDERSTANDING TROUT

Some knowledge of trout biology and behavior brings both greater appreciation to your sport and more fish to net. Here are a few highlights to help your fishing, but as you progress you'll probably want to explore some of the more detailed references listed in Sources & Resources at the back of the book.

66 Of the many species of fish, each has its own special appeal, but none has the universal charisma of the trout...of all fish, the trout demands the most of the angler...and gives the most in return. 99

— Joe Brooks (1972)

### Water Temperature

Water temperature is important. All trout generally prefer water temperatures less than 70 degrees Fahrenheit, and will usually seek out cooler tributaries and underwater springs as rivers and ponds warm in the summer and early fall. In general, most trout will feed most actively at water temperatures between 50 and 65 degrees. While trout can survive in near-freezing water, temperatures of 80 degrees and higher are usually lethal.

## Memory

Like most animals, trout can learn and remember — a kind of behavioral conditioning that means the same trout won't keep whacking at the same fly pattern over and over again until it dies of old age. On crowded, heavily fished rivers where trout gain considerable experience with fishermen, this sometimes means that doing something different from most other anglers can be espe-

In ponds and lakes, trout frequent edges — along underwater weedbeds, where shallow water meets deep, at inlet and outlet channels — that harbor concentrations of the insects they eat. Concentrate your efforts on such edges.

cially important. On Connecticut's Housatonic River, for example, I once caught an embarrassing number of trout by using a big, wiggly Woolly Bugger when other anglers were trying to fool the few rising trout with minuscule blue-winged olive drys.

Trout — especially larger ones

This angler, on a small Pennsylvania creek, is not praying for a strike, but keeping his profile low to improve his chances of success. Trout are easily frightened, so you must learn to sneak up on them.

— are easily frightened. They spend their lives learning to avoid predators — and that includes fishermen. You have to sneak up on them, which means moving slowly

and wading with as little water disturbance as possible. Sloppy casting scares trout, too; so take your time or you won't take your fish.

## Selectivity
Trout are often selective, meaning very fussy about not only fly pattern and size, but also how those flies are presented to the fish. Selectivity is primarily based on their vision, which as a general case in the trout's world is much better than yours. Trout are more sensitive to motion than any other visual input, which means that *subtle* twitches of your fly often add to its attractiveness. But don't overdo it.

## CATCHING STREAM TROUT
### First Moves
Before we get into the varied techniques of fly fishing in moving water, here's a nearly surefire, easy method that allows beginners to

## A TWITCH IN TIME

Remember that trout are more attuned to motion than any other potential sensory input, and use that fact to your advantage. Twitching your dry fly slightly on the surface makes that fly stand out from everything else — twigs, leaves — also floating on the river's currents. Trout often respond

well to this; sometimes even explosively — hitting your fly in a seeming fury.

The secret is in not twitching too much. A properly twitched dry will move an inch or two and then come to a dead stop. With few exceptions, yanking your fly across the surface 2 or 3 feet at a time is worse than useless and will often scare trout rather than attract them.

Stream fishing for trout means fishing the edges. In this case that means either the edge of the stream itself, where an undercut bank and the added protection of overhanging bushes make for a likely hide-out for a fish, or the edge between the main current and an eddy, where aquatic insects floating downstream are likely to be funneled toward waiting trout.

catch stream trout on a fly without even having to cast. Following these instructions exactly will often allow a few trout to be caught in any of America's diverse trout streams, even by complete novices.

## Tackle

We'll use most of the gear we started with in early chapters: a 6-weight rod between 8 and 9 feet long, and a single-action fly reel set up with a WF-6-F line. Any other properly matched size combination will also work. You'll want a 5X tippet, so either attach a 9-foot, 5X leader to your line or add a couple of feet of 5X tippet material to the

3X leader with which you rigged your fly line in Chapter 3.

## The Fly

Use a #14 or #16 Hare's Ear nymph, which is widely available, probably America's most popular nymph pattern, and generally imitative of many nymphs in all trout streams worldwide. Do not use one larger than #14; smaller is better in this case.

## The Water

Find a location in your area trout stream where the water is:
1. Knee-deep.
2. Tumbling over rocks or gravel into the upstream end or head of a

# Hypothetical Trout Stream

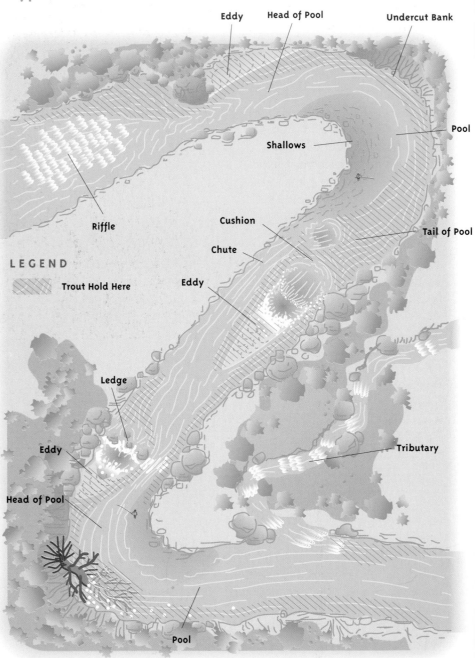

Eddy

Head of Pool

Undercut Bank

Pool

Shallows

Riffle

Cushion

Chute

Tail of Pool

LEGEND

Trout Hold Here

Eddy

Ledge

Eddy

Tributary

Head of Pool

Pool

Stretch of a hypothetical trout stream showing the various sorts of edges that fish tend to favor because they provide a combination of food and shelter. Note that in trout fishing, a pool is any stretch of a stream where the current slows somewhat either because the channel is deeper or wider.

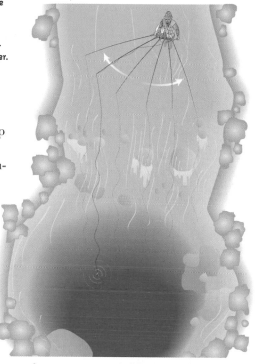

deeper pool.

Having rigged up, stand in the knee-deep water above the pool. Strip about 25 feet of line off the reel and wiggle the rod back and forth horizontally to get that line out through the rod guides and into the current in front of you. The current will straighten the line in front of you, carrying the leader and fly into deeper water and over the trout. Now — IMMEDIATELY — use your left hand to put the line under your right index finger, which will in turn clamp the line against the rod grip (for right-handed fisherman).

Now, slowly move the rod to the right or left. This makes the current move the line to the right or left also, which means your nymph is slowly moving in the current and just under the surface. At this point — or any

### First Moves: Fishing a Nymph Downstream

You've tied a #14 nymph imitation to your tippet. In midstream, having stripped 25 feet of line off the reel and allowed the current to take it downstream, you slowly move the rod to the right or left. This makes the fly move alluringly just below the surface. Get ready for a quick tug. You have hooked your first trout.

## GEAR TALK

### WHICH ROD?

Your 6-weight, 8- to 9-foot rod is the all-around trout rod. But it's too light for heaving giant streamer flies on really big trout water, which calls for an 8-weight. Conversely, a 6-weight is too heavy for a quiet spring creek or calm trout pond; that large a line just hits the water too hard, scaring fish. In such cases you'll want to go down to a 4-weight — even lighter if there's no wind and you're an accomplished caster.

time soon —
you may feel a
quick tug. A
trout! When
that happens
you need to
raise the rod
with your arm
to set the
hook. A quick,
violent wrist
snap here will
probably
break the
tippet, while

being too slow
means you'll
miss the fish.
Practice

When a trout strikes, you need to raise the rod with your arm to set the hook. Too violent a yank here could snap the tippet, while too cautious a response means you'll miss the fish. Only experience will teach you the right touch and bring results like the large rainbow (opposite).

makes perfect, so be prepared to miss some fish. Everybody does sometimes, no matter how skilled.

When you do hook a fish, wade to quieter water near the bank and retrieve the fish by stripping line in with your left hand from behind the right-index-finger grip. Don't pull too hard too fast; you'll break the leader. If the trout is a small one — like most trout — just slide your hand down the leader, grasp the fly, and twist it free, letting the trout go. If the fish is large and pulling strongly, let it pull line

## GEAR TALK

### NEED A NEW LINE?

Eventually your floating fly line will start to sink in fishing. The first answer is dirt, so try cleaning your line as described on page 42. If that doesn't help, you probably need a new line.

The plastic coating of most fly lines becomes brittle over a period of several seasons and starts to crack. This allows water to wick into the line's braided core, making the line less buoyant. Stepping on the line, dragging it over gravel, and leaving it on the hot dashboard of a sunlit car all hasten this process.

Changing flies during a caddisfly hatch on the Bighorn River, Montana. When confronted with a major hatch and plenty of trout hungrily rising to them, even experienced fishermen sometimes lose their cool. Remain focused, and don't fail to change fly sizes or even patterns if the fish are ignoring your fly.

from the reel, while winding line back in when the fish is pulling less strongly. Always keep some tension on the line; allowing slack may cause the hook to fall free before you've landed the fish.

Moving the fly *slowly* through the water back and forth with your rod will eventually cover a large stream area. Then take a couple of steps downstream and repeat the process, leaving the line extended in the water all the while. Congratulations. You're fly fishing — and fishing well — for trout even if you haven't learned how to cast yet!

66 To tell the truth, if I knew
all erbout fishin' fer trout,
I wu'd give it up an' tackle
sunthin' more int'resting. 99

— Arthur MacDougall (1946)

## WET FLIES AND NYMPHS

These are flies designed to be fished below the surface. They are generally representative of either drowned adult insects or partly emerged forms (wet flies) or else immature forms such as mayfly nymphs or caddis larvae (nymphs), some of which are present in both moving and still waters all year. Common sense dictates sometimes using a specific pattern to match a prevalent insect hatch; a small olive-colored nymph pattern on an afternoon when you've been seeing small, olive-colored mayflies on the water, for example. At other times, any small buggy-looking fly will do, such as the tried-and-true Hare's Ear nymph or a Leadwing Coachman wet fly. In most cases, small — meaning sizes 14-20 — is better because the majority of aquatic insect species are likewise small. Using too large a fly — with no specific reason for doing so other than convenience — is a common beginner's fault.

Common sense dictates using a specific fly pattern to match a prevalent insect hatch. But there are times when trying something different works. Fly Patterns: The GOLD-RIBBED HARE'S EAR NYMPH (bottom) is imitative of many aquatic insects, while the ROYAL COACHMAN WET (top) resembles none at all. Both are classic patterns that have proved their worth over generations of anglers.

These flies are most commonly fished down and across, which simply means casting at an angle across the current in a downstream direction. The fly will then swing around below you and is then either gently retrieved for a short distance and/or cast once again. Following the path of the drifting line and fly with your lowered rod tip is critical. If you don't, a large, curved belly will form in the drifting line, causing it — and the fly — to swing rapidly across the current. This is the most common mistake, which usually moves the fly too fast for the fish.

In late spring, summer, and fall, when trout are often feeding aggressively near the surface, a floating line will do. On big water or during times of early-season cold water when trout are near the bottom, you may need a full-sinking or sink-tip line to get your fly deeper.

## STREAMER FLIES

These are flies designed to look like

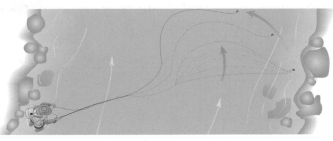

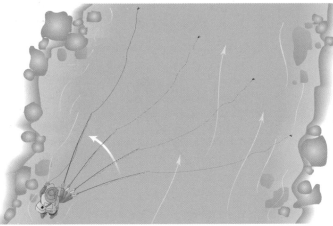

## Fishing Wet Flies & Nymphs Down & Across

When fishing wet flies and nymphs down and across the current, it is essential, once the fly has hit the water, to follow the drifting line and fly with your lowered rod tip (bottom). Failure to do so, a common mistake, causes a belly to form in the line as it is pulled downstream (top), and this drags the fly, pulling it faster than the current, a giveaway to the trout that something is amiss.
Fly Patterns: GRAY GHOST (top), MUDDLER MINNOW (bottom), ADAMS (opposite).

less the Muddler Minnow, which can be effective in sizes ranging from a humongous 2/0 down to a tiny #12. When in doubt, go medium (#6) to small.

Streamers are also commonly fished down and across like wets and nymphs, one difference being that streamers need to be twitched or stuttered in the current to imitate the darting motions of most bait fish. Accomplish this motion by raising and lowering your rod tip while — if you can — watching your fly. Not too fast, not too slow — and always enticing. Streamer flies are a searching method, often used to cover the stream when the trout aren't rising or — by specialists — in deliberately seeking larger fish. Strikes obtained by this method can be violent,

small fish. Since big fish inevitably eat small ones, streamers are known as big-fish flies. The success of streamer flies depends partly on the design or pattern of the fly of the moment, but most importantly on how you move the fly in the water: It *must* behave like a small fish. Our most widely used streamer is doubt-

which calls for leader tippets no smaller than 3X except for really miniature streamer patterns. Remember: That enticing, erratic fly movement is what attracts the predatory trout.

## DRY FLIES

These are flies designed to float, representing adult insects on the water's surface. There are three primary types.

## Mayflies

You'll sometimes see these on the surface as they emerge from their aquatic nymphal forms and gather enough warmth from the air to fly off. The colder the day, the longer these flies will drift on top of the water. They look like small sailboats — delta-shaped wings held paired and upright above slim bodies ending in two or three long, fine tails. The timing of their seasonal hatches is concentrated by species, each of which generally hatches during approximately the same calendar interval on the same stream from year to year. The popular Adams dry fly is a generic imitation of many small, drab mayflies and will often work when used in the appropriate size and you don't have a better, hatch-matching pattern.

# T E C H N I Q U E   T I P

### RELEASING TROUT

The easiest way to release small — meaning most — trout is to simply slide your hand down the leader, grasp the fly, and twist it from the fish's jaw without removing the fish from the water.

If you must grasp the trout, do so gently, trapping it against your body if needed to keep it from wiggling rather than squeezing it hard, which can be lethal. Larger trout will be landed most quickly with a net, in which case the fish can stay in and be controlled by the net as you remove the fly.

If the trout has been played hard — common with larger fish — hold the fish gently head first in the current, allowing it time to recover before you release your hand. A recovered trout will swim free of your hand of its own accord.

The caddisflies' rapid movement often elicits splashy, slashing rises from the trout, a behavioral clue you can use as a fly-choice indicator. The most widely used caddis drys are Elk Hair Caddis, a high-floating style that can be twitched on the surface to imitate the adults' movement.

## Terrestrials

These are land-based insects — ants, beetles, grasshoppers, and the like — that fall to the surface of the water and become prey for trout. Ants are the most important, and the most important thing in ant patterns is usually that they be small — typically size 18 or 20 and even smaller. A black ant made with two lumps of black fur dubbing and just a turn or two of hackle at the mid-section is the most effective, common pattern. A favorite fly for summer and early-fall fishing.

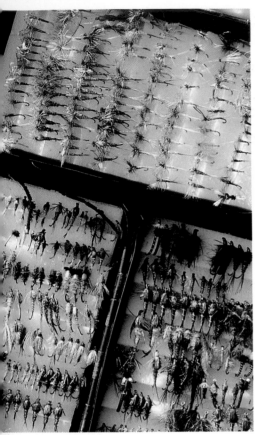

A well-stocked fly box containing a range of sizes and patterns of nymphs and dry flies, all to imitate mayflies. Fly Pattern: ELK HAIR CADDIS.

## Caddisflies

Another widely abundant insect group important to trout. They differ from mayflies in having their wings folded down along their backs in a distinct V or tentlike shape. They are also more active, commonly skittering along on the water's surface. They also have an erratically rapid flight pattern in the air, while mayflies tend to a more steady flight.

## FISHING DRY

There are numerous possibilities, many of them complex. The big problem is overcoming what's called drag — which is an unnatural movement of your floating fly caused as the intervening currents tug on the line. Here's a relatively simple solution.

Carefully wade to within about 40 feet of a rising trout. Plan your

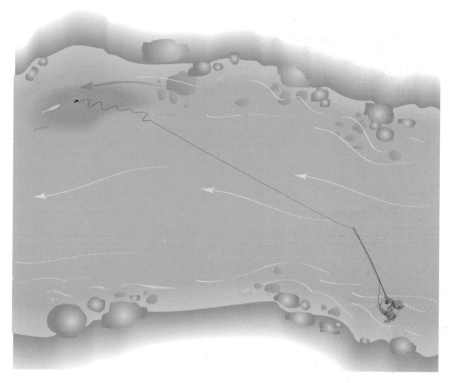

## First Moves: Fishing a Dry Fly Down & Across

Having quietly waded to within 40 feet of a rising trout, aim to place your fly about 3 feet upstream of the fish. On your final forward cast, stop your rod abruptly. This will cause the leader to recoil, leaving some slack near the fly and allowing a drag-free drift right over the hungry trout.

movements so the trout will be downstream and across from your casting position; roughly 45 degrees down and across if you need a measurement. Aim at a spot about 3 feet upstream of the rising fish. On your final forward cast, stop your rod *abruptly* and fairly high — about 45 degrees or a little higher. This abrupt stop will cause the leader and fly to recoil slightly in the air before landing, which will leave some slack in the leader near the fly. This slack should allow sufficient drag-free drift, but feel free to

66 The reason that all other kinds of fishermen look up to the dry-fly purist is not that he catches more fish than they; on the contrary, it is because he catches fewer. His is the sport in its purest, most impractical, least material form. 99

— William Humphrey (1978)

A Royal Trude dry fly riding high on the water. The points to keep in mind about the confounding number of patterns available are that a relative few will nearly always perform well, but when they don't, you must be prepared to try something new and different. See Chapter 14 for a list of the author's favorite flies.

experiment to get things just right.

If the fish refuses your fly, don't rip the line off the water immediately to try again. Let the current swing things around away from the fish first, then you won't scare it as you start your second cast.

### KEEP IN MIND

- Trout are wild creatures. You have to sneak up on them.
- Within a trout stream, fish are found along edges of things.
- Mayflies have upright sail-like wings; caddisfly wings are down and tentlike.
- More trout are spooked by sloppy, splashy wading than any other factor.
- Fish slowly and with careful observation; let the trout teach you what works.

# FLY FISHING FOR BASS

There are largemouth bass lurking beneath the lily pads in ponds from Maine to California, ready to rock and roll all over your floating bass bug at the merest twitch of your line. The smallmouth bass hunting crayfish around rock piles in a clear New Hampshire lake will also come to a fly readily, just like the smallmouths in a meandering Ozark river.

Black bass are ubiquitous, found in at least some of the warmer waters of almost every state. They are commonly caught on small lures at the surface, are sometimes easily fooled, and jump with abandon when hooked. All of which adds up to an ideal fly-rod fish.

## TYPES OF BASS

Largemouth bass are the most widely distributed, frequenting everything from small farm ponds to huge reservoirs nationwide. Largemouths are also found in the still backwaters of larger, warm river systems but are typically absent in areas with substantial current. Fish grow largest in warm southern regions with correspondingly longer growing seasons, but even northern fish can occasionally attain weights of 8 to 10 pounds. The average catch, however, is typically small, usually about a foot long in smaller, sheltered waters that offer the best fly fishing.

Smallmouth bass are typically a

Bass hang out in or near physical structures, whether they be underwater tree stumps or undercut banks or, as here, a group of lily pads. Placing your popping bug up against such a structure in the right season at the right time of day almost ensures an explosive strike.

little smaller than their largemouth cousins, often found in somewhat cooler lakes and cool, flowing rivers, and often associated with areas of underwater rock piles or ledges that are home to crayfish — a favored food

66 Although my enthusiasm for trout fishing and my fondness for the dry fly...are as long-standing as my bass experience, I esteem the bass and am always heart-stricken by the blasphemy against them so often expressed by rabid trout fishermen.99

— Ray Bergman (1942)

item. A 4-pound smallmouth is a big one anywhere, and typical catches are, again, a foot long or less in both rivers and lakes.

There's a handful of other American freshwater bass species, such as spotted and Guadalupe basses, but these are very limited in distribution and of comparatively little importance.

## UNDERSTANDING BASS
As with trout, understanding bass biology and behavior brings considerable rewards. It's that sort of knowledge that allows fly fishers to take bass consistently at many times regardless of state or location.

### Structure
Bass commonly relate to physical

structure in any body of water. That's a real key, and simply means that bass will most likely be found under or near some object — a bankside stump, a group of lily pads, a boat dock, an underwater ledge or rock pile — rather than being randomly dispersed in open water. For the wading fisherman or one in a small boat, this means casting to targets — placing your bass bug as closely as possible to any

Largemouth bass, the most widely distributed of all freshwater game fish, are found in little farm ponds (like this one in Pennsylvania) to huge lakes nationwide.

object or formation that might harbor a bass. Understanding this will save you much needless — meaning fruitless — casting over open water.

## Patterns

The patterning concept emerged from bass tournaments beginning in the 1970s as more and more fishermen started to realize that most of

the bass in a given body of water are behaving in similar ways at similar locations at any given day and hour. For example, if you're catching lots of bass in 5 to 8 feet of water off a rocky point on a particular day, other rocky points of the same depth should offer similar results — barring a radical weather change. More simply, if you catch a bass in a par-

*acts* like food. This is why a cardinal rule in bass fishing is often a slow retrieve, twitching a surface bug an inch or two at a time when a rapid retrieve would immediately brand your offering as phony. You have to assume the bass is interested, and you

Smallmouth bass are found in cool lakes as well as in cool, flowing rivers. They are more likely than largemouths to jump free of the water and tail-walk in an effort to throw your fly. Fly Patterns: Two common hard-body popping bugs that do well on bass (opposite).

ticular spot, similar spots become the most likely targets.

have to give the fish time to look things over.

## Curiosity

When a bass hears something hit the water with a gentle *plop*, it often swims over to investigate. This could be food, after all. Typically, the bass will then remain motionless under or near the floating bug for a minute or two, waiting to see if that bug then

## Timing Your Fishing

While it's often possible to catch bass at any time of day or night, the fish usually feed most actively at dawn and dusk. Dawn is especially productive, all the more so on summer-resort lakes that are chewed up by motorboats and water skiers during the day. From the

## GEAR TALK

### HOOK GAP

Hook gap means the distance between the hook's point and the fly's body just above it. Some bass bugs have too little space here, which makes hooking fish difficult. Make sure your bass bugs have adequate gap, which means generally matching that shown on the bass flies in Chapter 14.

first hint of light until the sun fully hits the water is prime time — however difficult for you — and a genuine must for those seeking larger fish.

## Spawning Time

Spawning bass are in shallow water, easily spotted and especially vulnerable to fly fishers at this time. Both largemouth and smallmouth females build circular depressions — "nests" — in the lake or river bottom, which are usually visible as lighter patches against a surrounding dark background and are usually in water less than 6 feet deep. Spawning may occur as early as April in southern states, while northern fish typically spawn between mid-May and mid-June. Bass remain on or near the nest guarding eggs for a week or two, and will often respond quickly to fly-rod offerings. Many states allow catch-and-release fishing during spawning season, which is often the best fishing of the year.

## BASS FLY TYPES

Bass flies are simply divided into surface and subsurface varieties that relate to the bass's opportunistic feeding habits. Unlike stream trout, which may concentrate on a specific insect hatch, bass tend to eat whatever happens along. This includes everything from frogs and small baitfishes to baby muskrats and small birds. Obviously, if the smallmouths along a rocky reef are feeding heavily on crayfish, which is common, then a crayfish pattern is appropriate. But in general, bass fishers have greater latitude in successful fly-pattern choices.

## Surface Flies

These are commonly called bass

---

## GEAR TALK

### FLY COLOR

Both largemouth and smallmouth bass can be exceptionally selective to fly color, even if that fly otherwise looks like nothing else on this earth. Black is good after dark; blends of yellow, red, and green are all-purpose daytime colors. All-yellow flies are sometimes effective, as is — so help me — bright purple. Experimenting with different bug colors is often a must on days when the fish seem fussy.

Swimming frog deer hair bass bugs. Once the fly has hit the water, let it sit still until all of the ripples it created die. Then twitch it gently and hold your breath. An explosive strike may ensue. Fly Patterns: opposite, clockwise from top — MUDDLER MINNOW, CLOUSER CRAYFISH, BLACK WOOLLY BUGGER.

softness of which may cause the bass to retain the bug longer on a strike, thereby increasing your hookups. The deerhair will become waterlogged over time, however, and start to sink — bugs, are often delightfully garish, and usually feature soft hackle feathers and/or rubber legs to add appealing wiggle. Some have flat or cupped faces that create chugs and gurgles when the bug is moved on the water. These are called poppers. Others are more subtle, often with a tapered front to move quietly on the water, and are called sliders.

Some derive their flotation from a spun deerhair body, the relative a disadvantage that will have you changing to a dry bug more often. The equally common alternative is a bug with a cork or foam body, which will float indefinitely. I often wind up using both styles, but more as a matter of whim than necessity.

Remember that the bigger the bass bug, the more difficult it will be to cast because of the bug's air resistance and weight. Smaller bugs, on the other hand, may be too

## CASTING FROM A BOAT

Two fishermen commonly work bass water from the same boat, and this presents some logistical problems if they're both fly casting.

The simplest solution is to cast one at a time. I'll fish out my cast on the water while you're casting in the air and vice versa, for example. That way we won't tangle. And yes, I'll watch what I'm doing when I do cast. Although I still don't see why you don't want me to bury a hook in your neck with my inattentive backcast!

small to elicit any interest. Small-mouths typically prefer smaller bugs than largemouths. Sizes 2 through 8 are common, with 6 being a good initial choice for typical small-pond conditions.

## Subsurface Flies

Here again, choices can be simple. You'll need some baitfish-imitating flies, and your trout-fishing streamer flies will do in a pinch. Muddler Minnows, for example, are also excellent bass flies. Many bass streamers are larger and bulkier, however, often with deerhair heads and soft, marabou wings to add wiggle. Some crayfish patterns are a must when fishing deep for small-mouths, which also tend to turn themselves inside out in their eager-

ness for a weighted and wiggly Black Woolly Bugger. One other style is long and wiggly, sort of like a small eel. I call these "worm flies," an oxymoron in the extreme, but there's no widely accepted name for this style. This is the fly fisher's answer to plastic worms, in which case the wing may be made of long, slim hackle feathers or a long strip of rabbit hide with the fur still attached.

## CASTING AND FISHING

There's nothing unusual about fly casting for bass, although the air resistance of larger flies may require that you slow down your casting stroke. The most important things happen at the completion of the cast.

Let's say we're fishing a small pond for largemouths in the evening from my canoe. Happily the wind

## FISHING DEEP

I should quickly point out that an experienced man fishing plastic worms is going to fish rings around any bass fly rodder — at least most of the time, and most especially when the bass are in deep water of 10 feet or more. You

can fish deep for bass with sinking lines and streamers, but that's a lot of work. Most of the fun in bass fly rodding is a smashing strike on the surface. So when the bass are deep, I either switch to non-fly gear or wait until dawn or dusk when fish are most likely to be in the shallows.

When fly casting from a boat, the simplest way to avoid entanglements or a hook in your partner's ear lobe is to cast one at a time.

isn't blowing, so sitting in one spot is easy. There's a large stump about 40 feet away and flanked by lily pads close to shore; an obvious target.

We'll aim to place our surface bug an inch or two from the stump. As the final forward cast unrolls, follow the line all the way down to the water with your rod tip and get the line under your right index finger as soon as the bug hits the surface. Now you're in immediate control, rod tip at water level with a straight fly line between you and the bug. Bass sometimes whack a bug almost instantaneously, and if you're not in quick control, you'll miss.

No strike yet, but there will be. Believing just that is half the battle. Let the bug sit still until the ripples from its landing have disappeared; as long as a full minute. Remember that a curious fish is probably sitting right next to it. Keep

  ❝ Even today, some Maine residents scorn bass as a tourist fish. Oh, bass are all right, I guess, a resort owner told me in 1970. There's a man over in Portland who eats the damned things! ❞

— Charles Waterman (1981)

your rod tip down near the water, just in case. Now use your left hand to sharply pull in 6 inches of line from behind your right hand. Don't move the rod tip upward! This creates slack and is a major, common mistake. Let the bug sit. Move it again. Sit. Move. WHAM!

When the bug disappears in a major-league swirl, raise the rod sharply. Bass have hard mouths, and considerable hook-setting force is usually necessary, even with very sharp hooks. Keep the rod up, line under control, and work the fish toward you by stripping line with your left hand. Bass don't run long distances like big trout sometimes do, but they will head hard for cover, potentially wrapping your line around lily-pad stems or a log. You'll have to counteract this, which with a really big bass will be difficult to impossible.

The Potomac and other large, middle-Atlantic rivers are typically top smallmouth-bass destinations.

## Landing Your Fish

Neither largemouths nor small-mouths have sharp teeth, which makes them easy to land. Grab the fish's lower jaw by putting your thumb in the fish's mouth and your fingers under the outside of the jaw. Bass lifted in this manner are more

# GEAR TALK

### BASS FLY RODS

Bass flies are typically large and air resistant, which has several implications for rod choice. It's harder to move these big bugs through the air, so a heavier line of greater mass than used in trout fishing is helpful. This means 8-weight or greater. A slow rod action helps, too, because casting these big bugs depends more on line mass than velocity. A big, slowly unrolling loop will allow the line to carry the fly. Choose a rod described as slow-actioned in a catalog or ask your salesman specifically for a rod of this type.

or less para-
lyzed, which
makes hook
removal and
fish releasing
simple.

## Varied Retrieves

Some bass
anglers prefer
to work their
poppers fairly
quickly in a
near steady
*chug-chug-
chug* that
leaves a trail of
bubbles across
the pond. Fast
retrieves some-
times trigger
equally rapid
strikes, per-
haps con-
vincing the
bass that some struggling food item
is about to escape. At other times, a
fast retrieve simply scares fish.

But the real secret — and one
that goes well beyond bass fishing
— is simply in varying your
retrieve until you encounter a
method that seems to work best at
that particular day and time. When

Bass flies are large and air resistant, which means that to successfully throw
them you'll need at least an 8-weight rod, but preferably a 9-weight. Keep
false casting to a minimum, concentrating instead on pulling the bug off
the water from your last cast, back-casting just once, and putting the bug
back on the water several yards from the last spot.

**?**

**DID YOU KNOW**
Black bass, meaning largemouths and smallmouths, are
America's number one gamefish, sought by some 13 million
anglers annually. Panfish are
second at 10 million, while
trout are a close third, targeted
by 9 million people every year.

Successful bass fishing means trying something
new whenever the action slows or stops. Simply
changing the pace of your retrieve often lands
results like this big largemouth. Remember,
experiment by going gradually from the slowest,
quietest retrieve to faster, splashier retrieves.

Bass have hard mouths, which means you must set the hook with real authority. It also means releasing the fish without damaging it is easy. Holding a bass by its lower jaw, with your thumb inside its mouth, virtually paralyzes it, a boon to amateur photographers.

you experiment, try the least intrusive, quietest retrieve first to avoid scaring fish. If that doesn't work, try stripping line faster or more erratically. Vary your rhythm, too. On some days bass will come only to streamers stripped in a reggae beat, while on other days they'll only hit poppers played in waltz time.

### KEEP IN MIND

- Bass are curious and like to look things over. Let your floating bug sit still for a minute or even longer when first cast while the fish decides.
- Cast your bass flies around structures like stumps and boat docks rather than fishing open water.
- Slow retrieves are usually best, but don't be afraid to experiment with retrieve speeds.

# PANFISHES
# AND
# PIKES

The term "panfish" generally refers to sunfishes and perch, the fish of barefoot boys and bent pins, of farm ponds and summer afternoons. But they're also a wonderful fly fisher's fish, as worthy of elegant fishing rods as they are of simple fishing poles. And perhaps most worthy in the kitchen as virtually all panfishes are both prolific and exceptional food fish.

## SUNFISHES

There are more than twenty different species of North American sunfish, many with colorful names such as long-ear, pumpkinseed, and bluegill.

The fish themselves are colorful, too, often with bright orange bellies blending upward through metallic greens and yellows to deep blue-green backs. They seem at first to be oddly compressed — roughly the same shape as an English muffin — with fins, short tail, and a small, pugnacious-looking, turned-up jaw. But that shape is ideal for quick darts and agile turns among shallow strands of waterweed, an agility necessary both in feeding on small fish and insects and in trying to escape the engulfing maw of a largemouth bass, which commonly feeds on sunfish.

Bluegills are the most common and widely distributed, and the oldest

bluegills build nestlike depressions in the shallow margins of ponds and lakes where their light-colored saucers are highly visible. They are similar to the closely related basses in this habit, but use much shallower water and their nests are closer

Use a small (#10) version of a hard-bodied floating bass bug to catch bluegills, an ideal fly-rod target that can be taken on light trout tackle.

and wisest of these sunnies may rarely attain weights of 3 pounds or more. Typically, though, a 10-incher is a giant, with 6 to 8 inches being most common. Their shallow-water abundance coupled with a hard fight and a willingness to take a wide variety of small flies make them an ideal fly-rod target when sought with light trout tackle.

In late spring, spawning

together. Sunnies are very aggressive at this time — even pecking at the legs and feet of an angler who wades too close — and will readily take any small trout fly or bug, dry or wet. Later in the summer as waters warm, larger bluegills often retreat to deeper water. At this time, a small, size 10-14 nymph fished between 6 and 12 feet deep on a sinking line along weedy margins usually fills the bill.

## T E C H N I Q U E    T I P
### BLUEGILL BUGS

These specialized flies are miniature versions of popular, hard-bodied floating bass bugs. Size 10 is good for starters. Fish slowly as you would for bass. Bluegills take more quietly than bass, often with a kisslike smack instead of a broad swirl. Pinch down the barb on your hook to make releasing large numbers of fish easier.

Panfishing, Saint John's River, Florida. Crappies feed on minnows, which means a size 8 or 10 streamer fished on a sinking line along the margins of weed beds or near submerged brush should work well.

## CRAPPIES

Another member of the sunfish family, crappies grow somewhat larger, often reaching 2 pounds or a little more. They are often an elegant pale green with a vertical barring of black or dark gray. They are a Middle America fish, originally found from Lake Ontario south through Texas and east to North Carolina, but have become more widely established in ponds and reservoirs through stocking.

Crappies are best known as minnow feeders, which makes a size 8 or 10 White Marabou streamer fished

## WATCH FOR SPINES

All the panfishes I've described have sharp dorsal spines concealed in their dorsal fin along the top of their backs. This means a painful hand puncture for the unwary. To handle these fish safely, hold the leader in your left hand with the fish dangling in the air. Slide your right hand down the fish's back — starting at the head — which will fold down both dorsal fin and spines and allow you to then grasp the fish firmly for unhooking.

## THE PERCHES

Both yellow and white perch — our two common species — are incredibly prolific and exceptional eating. They're my personal favorite in that regard, and while I catch-and-release many different species for sport, in fishing for food I fish for perch. They are, to borrow from Walton, "too good for any but anglers, or very honest men."

The perches are extremely prolific in ponds and lakes across North America. Thanks to their numbers, and their willingness to take a fly, they often provide children with their first exhilarating catch.

### Yellow Perch

Their overall butter-yellow color sharply marked with dark vertical bars makes these perch easily recognizable, as does the bright orange tint to their fins. An 8- to 12-incher is a good fish in most ponds and lakes, although yellow perch will rarely weigh as much as 3 pounds. Perch school for spring spawning in the shallow margins and

on a sinking line near their favored submerged brush piles ideal. They are a schooling fish, which means that finding and catching one is usually the key to catching several more. In summer's hot weather, crappies may move to deep water and beyond the reach of conventional fly tackle.

A very nice yellow perch. These fish are so numerous and so delicious that they put even the most conscientious catch-and-release advocates to the test.

bays of many lakes, when they can be taken in considerable numbers. In summer, they'll often move into 8 to 12 feet or more of water, when you'll need a sinking line. Any small, bright, wet fly or streamer will often work in sizes from 8 down to 12. A distinct start-and-stop darting retrieve has — for me at least — produced the most fish.

## White Perch

Similar in shape to yellow perch, although perhaps more chunky, white perch otherwise look quite different. Color is a solid silver-gray with pale tints of green and yellow blending to a dark green-gray back. Those catching one of these fish for the first time often consider them to be a small, oddly colored bass. These are generally an eastern and northern fish, although established elsewhere by stocking. They are most commonly encountered by fly anglers when a school of deep-water lake perch moves inshore during the evening, rising to insects on the calm surface during the last hour of light. Trout dry flies often work at such times, and the evening perch rise

**DID YOU KNOW**
Rod or Pole? This is a matter of definition. If it cost less than $10, it's a fishing pole. More than $10, it's a fishing rod.

can be the tasty highlight of a day otherwise spent trolling or casting for trout, salmon, or smallmouth bass in a northern lake.

Another bluegill taken on the Saint John's River, Florida. When releasing bluegills, take care to avoid cutting yourself on their sharp dorsal spines.

## THE PIKES

Your first impression will be of teeth — big, sharp teeth. And if you're careful, that impression will be only mental. More than one novice has wound up with bloody, sore hands from trying to unhook a pike or pickerel by hand rather than with long-nosed pliers, as is the commonsense rule. As fly fishing has continued to diversify in recent years, fly rodding for pike, which can reach 30 pounds and more, has become increasingly popular. Fly fishing for the related but

66 And the mighty sturgeon, Nahma, Said to Ugudwash, the sun-fish, To the bream, with scales of crimson, 'Take the bait of this great boaster, Break the line of Hiawatha!'99

— Henry Wadsworth Longfellow
(1859)

A hefty northern pike taken at Lake Beverly, Alaska. There is nothing dainty about these attack fish. With their rocketlike shape and speed and their razor-sharp teeth, they are worthy adversaries. Absent a landing net, grasp the fish firmly across the gill covers just behind the head.

Chain pickerel, the northern pike's smaller cousin, is found in the same warm-water lakes and ponds as largemouth bass. This one was taken on Lake Okeechobee, Florida.

## Chain Pickerel

Although reaching a maximum size of about 10 pounds and 3 feet long, most pickerel are much smaller, ranging from 14 to 24 inches with weights to 3 or 4 pounds. They are common in many warm-water lakes and slow-flowing streams, frequently in combination with largemouth bass, but are often not found in the same waters as their larger northern-pike cousins, with which they can be competitive. Large bright streamer flies — from 3 to 5 inches long — are most effective. Adding a short tippet of dark-colored wire will help prevent cutoffs, while an erratic retrieve will produce the most strikes.

smaller pickerel is essentially similar, so I'll consider the techniques together after looking at the fish themselves.

## Northern Pike

The fly-rod appeal of northern pike is elemental. Consider the trout fisherman who, after 20 years of trying, has yet to catch a trout longer than 18 inches. Now his guide has handed him a heavy, 10-weight fly rod and a streamer fly

## GEAR TALK

### WIRE LEADERS

In addition to special pike leaders with wire tippets that are sold ready-made, you can also use the same common tackle-shop wire leaders that spinfishermen use. These are wire with a snap on one end and a swivel on the other. Use black, 6-inch-long versions. Cut the barrel swivel from one end with wire cutters and tie your nylon leader to the remaining loop. Use the snap on the other end to attach your fly. Simple — and much less expensive than what you'll find in a fly shop.

bigger than the size of his average trout. So he casts and strips, casts and strips, along the margins of a Manitoba lake until suddenly an immense, submarine-like wake arrows toward the fly. There's a violent swirl; the guide shouts; and the angler babbles — incoherent and immobile — having been so incredibly shocked he forgot to tighten on the line. The fish is long gone, but pike fishing can be like that.

North American pike range from Labrador to Alaska and south into our northern states. While 40-pound-plus fish are theoretically possible, many anglers travel to remote northern waters in hopes of 30-pounders they never see, and anything over 25 pounds should be considered a lifetime fish. The majority of pike are 10 pounds or less, ranging from 36 inches down to 20 inches or less. But they are exciting fish at any size.

## The Nature of Pike

Pike and pickerel reveal their habits by their shape and coloration. They are long, slim fish with enlarged, propulsive fins at and near the tail — much like fins on a rocket. This basic design implies a sudden, rapid attack over a short distance and from a standing start. Their dark gray-green mottling over a green background matches perfectly the aquatic weeds in which they hover motionless, waiting for baitfish —

or your fly — to swim within their attack radius. I use the word "attack" on purpose; there's nothing dainty about pike.

## Pike Tackle

Pike respond best to big streamer flies. For trophy fish, this means the biggest fly you can cast with heavy gear — streamers in some combination of red, yellow, and/or white that are 6 inches long or more. Fly rods should be 9-footers of 9-weight and up, 11- or 12-weights for casting the biggest flies. Your weight-forward floating line should be of a "pike" or "bass" taper, which means there's a greater than usual weight-forward bias to help carry big flies in the air. A full-sinking line will get your fly down to the deeper weedbeds where pike are often found in hot weather. In any area where large fish are

66 I don't want to ketch no tarpon that weighs half a ton. And feedin' clams to sheepshead isn't just what I call fun. Of salmon when it's boiled or baked I'll say that I am fond — But when I'm after sport I fish for pick'rel in a pond. 99

— Norman Jeffries (1905)

possible, I use a heavy leader tapered to 15-pound-test, while 10-pound will do for small-fish water. The addition of a dark-colored wire tippet may mean somewhat fewer strikes, but definitely means more landings.

## Retrieves for Pike

The key word is erratic. Pike (and pickerel) often have to be teased into striking, and the steady, stripping cadence used by most streamer-fly anglers often won't do it. Vary the speed and cadence of your strips within a single cast. Talk to your fly, willing it to wiggle. Do a little dance. Sing. Whatever it takes to get you to make your fly dart, wiggle, stop, and mambo its way along the edge of a weedbed.

## Happy Landings

Always remember that both pike and pickerel sometimes allow themselves to be drawn near the boat with seeming docility, only to erupt in a surface-thrashing frenzy at the sight of the boat itself. More big pike are lost at this moment than at any other, so be ready.

A large boat net makes landing these fish much simpler, and it also helps control them for hook removal and release. Absent a net, you can grasp the fish by hand firmly across the gill covers just behind the head. Big pike are too large for this, in which case you'll have to grab the gill cover itself. Just make sure the fish is played out first. And remember those teeth!

### KEEP IN MIND

- Your medium to light trout tackle is perfect for all panfishes.
- Panfish have small mouths, meaning a #8 maximum fly size.
- All panfish are delicious and fecund, meaning you can almost always keep a few without hurting the population.
- Two pike/pickerel keys: big streamers, erratic retrieves.
- Land and release pike/pickerel with a net and long-nosed pliers.

# S A L T W A T E R
# N O R T H

It all seemed to happen at once. One minute I was standing on a coastal Rhode Island jetty, idly watching schools of juvenile herring swim past the rocks at my feet. A minute later, those same baitfish were skittering across the surface under a cloud of screaming, diving terns. There were long, dark shapes moving fast under the panicked herring, striped bass trapping baitfish against the rocks.

I cast a streamer fly just 20 feet out from the rocks, well beyond most of the fish, and watched the fly disappear in a broad swirl. The bass took the line hard and then settled down 50 feet out to a series of bulldogging tugs parallel to the jetty. I finally stepped down to a rock closer to the water, and eventually grabbed the bass by its lower jaw, slipping out the hook and watching the fish swim free. It was the kind of morning when everything goes right, payback time for hard, empty hours of no fish and learning the water. You pay your dues that way; we all do — and you then get your fish.

The popularity of saltwater fly fishing has grown enormously in recent years, partly because of reduced commercial fishing and a corresponding resurgence in populations of fish such as redfish or

In northern waters from Maine to North Carolina the striped bass is the most important target of fly rodders. Most shore-based fly-rod catches range between 2 to 12 pounds.

from Maine to North Carolina — striped bass are the most important fly-rod targets, although fly fishers will also encounter other species such as bluefish, northern weakfish, and even small tuna such as bonita.

As in freshwater fly fishing, understanding your quarry's behavior and habits will pay off handsomely in the salt. So before we head for the water, here's a look at the fish themselves.

channel bass in the south and striped bass in the north. Not only are there more fish to catch than there were 20 years ago, but prime fishing areas are often easily accessible — even without a boat — and near coastal population centers. In northern waters — and primarily

## STRIPED BASS

Stripers or "rockfish," as they're often called from Maryland southward, have been America's most important near-shore gamefish ever since a small band of pilgrims at Plymouth, Massachusetts, used their striper catches to avert starvation in the fall of 1623. Saltwater bass are generally slimmer overall than their distantly related fresh-

66 There is not a pleasanter summer day's amusement than a merry cruise after the Blue-Fish, no pleasanter close to it than the clambake, the chowder, and the broiled Blue-Fish, lubricated with champagne. 99

— Frank Forrester (1851)

While bluefish populations have been declining since the early 1980s, there is nothing as exciting as hooking one of these high-speed hunters as it herds schools of baitfish before it.

Striper fishing from a jetty, Barnegat Inlet, New Jersey. You'll tend to find fish where the water is both moving and deep enough to hold baitfish. A rocky jetty fished just before and after a high tide often satisfies both conditions.

water counterparts, but retain a broad body shape and large tail that gives extreme maneuverability at the expense of some speed. This reflects the striper's near-shore feeding habits, which include the uncanny ability to swim and feed accurately in the maelstroms of white water where crashing surf meets the shore. Female stripers may live as long as 30 years or more and reach weights to 125 pounds,

## GEAR TALK

### BARBLESS HOOKS

There's a little conservation involved here, but more self-preservation on the angler's part. All my northern saltwater flies are barbless because it makes me feel better about flinging these big stainless-steel harpoons back and forth past my neck. Sometimes I file away a hook's barb before tying the fly; otherwise I simply bend the barb down with pliers. Barbless also means it's much easier to release fish, most especially toothy bluefish that might otherwise bite my finger.

although most shore-based, fly-rod catches will range between 12 and 30 inches (2 to 12 pounds) with the ever-present potential for much larger fish. Striped bass spawn in major East Coast estuaries such as those of the Hudson and Delaware Rivers, and there are resident populations scattered from Maine to the Gulf Coast. The majority of bass, however, are spawned in the various tributaries of Chesapeake Bay, migrating north by inshore routes as far as Nova Scotia in the spring and returning in late fall.

## BLUEFISH

Through the 1970s and 1980s, voracious schools of bluefish were common along the Atlantic coast, but populations now seem to be declining. Overfishing — both recreational and commercial — is a probable cause, together with some still-unknown natural cycles that for several hundred years have been noted for periods of abundance broken by several decades of near invisibility. Bluefish are a fast-swimming, schooling fish noted for their ability to herd schools of baitfish into coves or against a beach, a scene that quickly turns into a surface-splashing and bloody melee as the big, blue-gray "choppers" slash right and left with piranha-like jaws — sometimes beaching themselves in their own frenzy. Bluefish commonly reach

---

### TECHNIQUE TIP
#### WIND

While the best fishing times of dawn and dusk are often windless and calm, ocean breezes at other times are a big problem. First and foremost, if it's blowing hard along the shore, either switch to spinning tackle or stay home studying this book and practicing your knots. Fly casting will be just too difficult.

Or choose your fishing spots with the wind in mind. One rocky point might offer you a tailwind that can actually be helpful in making longer casts, while the jetty a mile away might be angled in such a way as to require casting into the wind, which is difficult. Or try to keep the wind on your left cheek (for right-handed casters), in which case the airborne fly line will be blown away from your body as you cast. The worst case is a strong wind coming from your (right) casting side, blowing the line and fly toward you in the air. That's a recipe for a hook in the back of your neck. Be aware of that situation, and avoid it.

weights to 16 pounds, and fly fishing in the midst of such a "blitz" offers one of the greatest adrenaline rushes in all of angling.

## NORTHERN WEAKFISH

Another inshore, coastal migrant, weakfish generally resemble freshwater perch in shape, but with no vertical barring. Weakfish — so named for their soft mouths from which a hook will tear easily — reach weights to 17 pounds or more and lengths greater than 3 feet. They were common as recently as the 1970s from Massachusetts southward, but intense commercial harvesting of immature, juvenile weakfish from the Chesapeake through the Carolinas has dramatically reduced their availability to sport anglers. They are still occasionally encountered by fly rodders, usually when a few weakfish are mixed in with a school of feeding stripers.

## ATLANTIC BONITO

Schools of this fast-swimming, small tuna occasionally frequent

## A BASKET RETRIEVE

This specialized retrieve style avoids tangles and catches fish. I was first shown this years ago by saltwater veteran and friend Lou Tabory and have used this method successfully ever since. Make a long cast. When the cast lands on the water, put the rod grip well up under your right arm and use arm pressure to hold the rod grip against your body. Now you've got two hands free to slowly strip in the line hand-over-hand fashion directly into your stripping basket, varying the speed of the strips to suit fishy whims of the day. A strike will feel like a hard pull. Pull back on the line with your left hand while raising the rod with your right. Let the fish pull out any remaining slack so you can play the fish from the reel. And you're in business.

inshore waters as far north as Mass-achusetts between August and October, often associated or mixed with another tuna — the similar-appearing false albacore. Often called "bonita," these football-shaped torpedoes range upward to about 10 pounds and sometimes feed actively near jetties or inlets. Small tuna are unique in that their extreme speed and sharp eyesight often require fast, long casts; small, imitative streamer-fly patterns; and substantial backing as a hooked bonito can strip 200 yards of line in seemingly less time than it takes to read about it. The similar Pacific bonito is a common fly-rod target off the coast of southern California.

A stripping basket is essential gear for northern saltwater fly fishing.

## FINDING FISH

The ocean is a big place, and it seems all the more so when you're standing amid miles of beach armed with fly tackle that somehow seems very insignificant when con-fronted with all that water. Finding fish is the hardest part, but even this can be comparatively simple as you discover that striped bass, for

## T E C H N I Q U E   T I P
### STRIPING BASKETS

These are essential for the wading fly rodder in northern saltwaters. Without one, your slack casting line will tangle in rocks or in the surf. This inexpensive setup comes from your local hardware store. Use a RubberMaid dishpan with a hole drilled in each of two corners. The hooks of a bungee cord will fit in those holes, and the elastic cord will hold the basket around your waist. Do not drill drain holes in the basket bottom. If you do, it will fill with water when you wade deeply.

The fast-swimming Atlantic bonito, a tuna that ranges up to 10 pounds, can strip 200 yards of line off your reel in no time. Bonito require small flies, big reels, and big rods, preferably 11- or 12-weight models.

example, will be found only at certain places under certain circumstances — both of which are often predictable.

## Time and Tide

Inshore waters change dramatically in depth approximately every 6 hours as tides change from high to low, becoming high again about 6 hours later. Along the Connecticut shore, for example, this fluctuation amounts to 7 to 9 vertical feet of depth. Farther north the tidal change is greater, while being somewhat less as one progresses south. This does not occur at precise 6-hour intervals, but rather advances slightly each day, which makes a tide chart or similar reference essential. Tackle shops often have these, and the same information is often published daily in coastal newspapers.

This vast water movement influences the fish, of course, and a stretch of beach that held hundreds of feeding stripers in the morning may be bone dry in the afternoon. The same water movement also creates current as moving tides flow around points, rocky jetties, the narrow channels between islands, and in estuaries large and small. Gamefish favor such places because the currents often carry baitfish, shrimp, and other food. Ideally, then, you'll be looking for water that's deep enough to hold fish and that's moving at the same time. A long, rocky jetty fished from 2 hours before high tide until 2 hours after is a simple example that usually satisfies both conditions.

# GEAR TALK

### USE ENOUGH ROD

Big fish. Big flies. Big rod. That's it in a nutshell, and rod weights of 10 up to 12 are almost mandatory in northern saltwaters. Your 6-weight trout rod will do for small stripers on small streamers in small tidal creeks, but you can't cast really big flies with that rod, nor can you pull hard enough with it to land a bass of 20 pounds or more. Some rod makers tout 9-weights for stripers and blues, but I've tried them and they're too light, also. After 20 years of trying, I've settled on 11- and 12-weights with a medium to slow action as being ideal. The slower action is easier to cast hour after hour than a fast-actioned rod, while the rods themselves are sufficiently strong to give me a good pull on larger fish.

Shooting line toward a striper. The best all-around northern saltwater line is a very slow-sinking intermediate. Fly Patterns: POPOVIC'S SURF CANDY (opposite, top); ROGER'S SAND EEL (bottom).

## Timing Your Trip

The first hour of daylight is almost invariably the best time to seek both striped bass and bluefish. Both will come into very shallow water to feed after dark, and often feed voraciously for an hour or so as the sky first turns pink at dawn.

## GEAR TALK

### THE RIGHT LINE

While a floating, weight-forward saltwater taper is sometimes useful — in really shallow water after dark or in fishing surface poppers during the day, for example — the best all-around northern saltwater line is a very slow-sinking intermediate. Some of my lines, for example, are WF-11-I (weight-forward, 11-weight, intermediate). These slow-sinking lines get below the surface chop that tugs and pulls a floating line, which means the intermediate line keeps you in straighter contact with your fly — a big plus.

As an ideal case, you'll combine that timing with the right tide and the right location — incoming high tide on a jetty surrounded with baitfish schools, for example. That's about as close to a guarantee of fly-rod fish as there can be anywhere along the coast. As you gain experience, you'll start fishing after dark. Morning and evening are easier, however, just because you can see what you're doing.

On a seasonal basis, spring and fall are the best times as both striped bass and bluefish concentrate in near-shore migrations. Migrating stripers, for example, typically leave the Maine coast by early September, pass through Massachusetts and Rhode Island waters during October, and through November and early December are found along the New Jersey shore on their way to spend the winter in ocean waters off Hatteras. The reverse happens in spring, with migrations starting by mid-April and generally being complete by early July when summer-resident populations are established throughout the coast.

## FLIES

While there are myriad saltwater fly patterns and styles, the ones you actually *need* are relatively few.

First, you need streamer flies in four colors: white, for all-purpose, anytime fishing; black, for after dark; yellow, for when white doesn't work; and finally bright, fluorescent-dyed chartreuse, which for some reason will occasionally pull stripers and bluefish like no other color. This sounds almost too simple, but it works. Other colors may also work; none is more important, however.

## Fly Size

Size is critical. Unlike trout flies in which a given hook size defines overall fly size, saltwater streamers use usually made on a large hook with a long trailing wing. This works simply because most northern saltwater fish scarf up the whole thing on the strike anyway, so short strikes or fish nipping at the fly's tail are rarely a problem. The critical part is overall fly length, an attribute to which stripers and other fish can be exceptionally selective.

Stripers feeding on small silversides (a saltwater minnow) may demand a 3-inch-long fly, while the same fish taking larger sand eels (a slim, eel-like baitfish) in the fall may refuse everything that isn't 6 inches long. Bonita are the fussiest in this regard, and you'll want to try a 2-inch-long pattern when you first spot the rapid surface boils of a fast-moving school. The overall answer, then, is a selection of streamer flies 2, 3, 4, 5, and 6 inches long in each of the four basic colors. Hook sizes will typically range from 6 up to 1/0 or 2/0.

If the saltwater bug bites you, you'll soon find yourself investing in rods, reels, lines, and leaders specialized for the task. Fly Patterns: TABORY'S SLAB FLY (top), SKIPPING BUG (bottom)

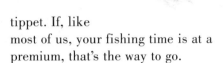

## LEADERS

These can be simple. I usually use 9-footers tapered to 12- or 15-pound-test at the tippet end. Really large stripers, meaning over 20 pounds, demand a short (say, 12 inches) section of heavy, so-called shock tippet of at least 30-pound-test nylon monofilament between leader and fly to protect against leader abrasion during a long fight. I usually don't bother with this, even knowing that someday my neglect may cost me a big fish.

The sharp teeth of bluefish require a short wire leader. There are many complex ways of rigging such a leader, but there's also one very simple route. Because of saltwater fly fishing's growing popularity, many coastal fly shops now sell leaders pre-rigged with wire

tippet. If, like most of us, your fishing time is at a premium, that's the way to go.

## PUTTING IT ALL TOGETHER

While many saltwater situations can demand booming casts to 80 feet and beyond, others — notably jetties — often require casting no more than 30 feet. There's one other short-cast situation within reach of novices, and that's the all-important outlet from a salt pond or marsh.

Salt ponds are common up and down the coast and vary widely in size from puddles to large lakes. Most are connected to the ocean by a narrow channel through which the tide flows like a river. And like trout in a river, stripers and other fish feed in this current, gulping

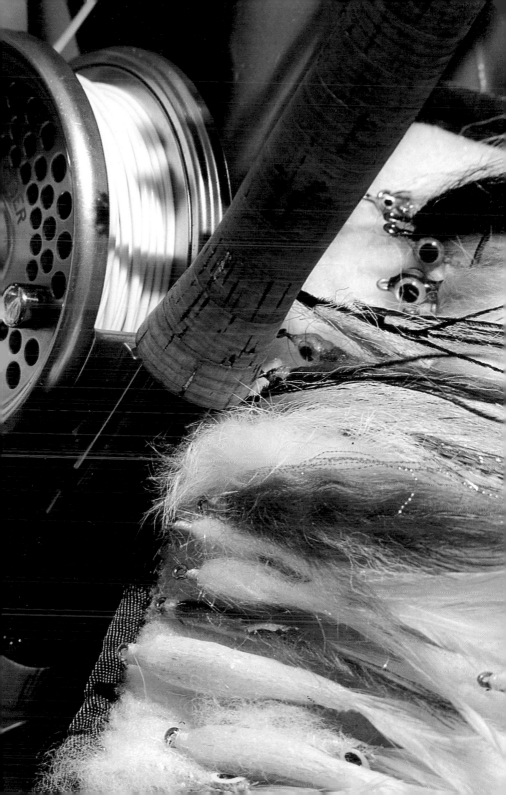

With northern saltwater fishing, time and tide are critical to success. The first and last hours of daylight are the best times to seek stripers and bluefish. Consult local tackle shops or tide charts to learn on which dates each month the tide changes near dawn or dusk.

baitfish and other food being swept from the pond toward the ocean.

There's an optimum combination of circumstances here, which is a high tide that starts going out at dawn. All you need do is find a pond with a saltwater outlet on a regional map. Show up in chest waders with your rod fully rigged at 5 a.m. high tide, being careful not to shine your flashlight out over the water, thereby scaring fish. As the tide changes and starts to flow outward, fish the outlet current with your streamer fly just like a trout stream. Long casts typically aren't required, and even a large striper may suddenly and shockingly smash your fly as close as your rod tip.

### KEEP IN MIND

- Best times for all fish are dawn and dusk.
- Plan your fishing with a monthly tide table.
- Use enough rod: 10-weights and heavier.
- Four basic streamer colors: white, black, yellow, and chartreuse.
- Use sharp, barbless hooks.

# SALTWATER
# SOUTH

Sunlight on sand is almost painful, especially when the sand is bright white and covered with 6 inches of water and you're trying to follow the dark shadow of a cruising and exceedingly spooky bonefish. Squinting, I finally saw the fish itself, bright silver and almost invisible through silver reflections on the water's surface. And I blew it. One bad cast hit the water too hard, and the fish was off like a shot, plowing a big furrow on the surface as it headed for distant deep water. Bonefishing is like that; the near misses keep you pumped, keep you coming back.

Fly fishing in tropical waters generally means from Florida and the Gulf Coast south through the Bahamas, Mexican coast, and Central America, where among many diverse gamefish species the most popular fly-rod targets are bonefish everywhere and redfish in our southern states. Both of these fish enter broad expanses of shallow water (called "flats") to feed, where they can be spotted by a wading angler who then carefully stalks the fish to get within casting range. This adds an element of hunting to the fishing experience, bringing new levels of excitement while also offering northern anglers an escape from abysmal weather back home.

In many areas, this fishing either

Redfish, also called channel bass, are found from the Carolinas south to Florida and the Gulf Coast. They can be spotted as they cruise shallow flats grubbing for crabs and shrimp.

thanks again to increasingly restricted commercial fishing. In Florida, for example, voters statewide approved a 1995 ban on most near-shore commercial fishing nets, a tribute to the economic importance of sportfishing that in the near term should increase populations of nearly all shallow-water gamefish species in addition to fishes such as mullet on which many other fish feed. Along the Texas Gulf Coast, meanwhile, commercial fishing for redfish was virtually eliminated a few years ago, thanks largely to work by the Gulf Coast Conservation Association. The resulting proliferation of redfish and other gamefish there has since been remarkable, making that coastal sport fishery a new hot spot that according to one study contributes $1 billion annually to that state's economy.

has gotten dramatically better in recent years or is soon to become so,

## GEAR TALK
### FEELING THE TAKE

Both bonefish and redfish sometimes present a curious problem. You're stripping line toward you, and the fish is following the fly, likewise toward you. The fish opens its mouth, takes the fly, and keeps swimming toward you at the same speed. In this case, you won't feel anything because the fish hasn't turned or otherwise put tension on the line. The answer is to make a slightly longer, faster strip when you think something might have happened. In that event you'll feel the fish if it has the fly and can then raise the rod to set the hook. If the fish hasn't taken yet, you won't take the fly completely away from it.

Among fly fishermen, the lightning-fast bonefish is the most sought after of tropical saltwater gamefish. Here an angler is poled toward cruising bonefish by a guide in Boca Paila, Mexico.

## REDFISH

Channel bass, red drum, and redfish are all one and the same fish, being known as bass or drum in the Carolinas and redfish in the west-Florida backcountry and along the Gulf Coast. Although redfish can reach 90 pounds, the best fly fishing is in shallow, protected waters from Everglades National Park and Florida Bay west along the Gulf Coast where fish of 1 to 6 pounds are abundant. Redfish are spotted as they cruise shallow, grassy bottomed flats or as they start feeding along shallow bars on a rising tide. The fish's habit of grubbing the bottom for crabs and shrimp often causes its waving tail to gently break water, and in calm weather those tails can be seen from several hundred yards distant. "Tailing" fish give a ready target that can be stalked by slow-moving

boat or by wading, circumstances depending.

## BONEFISH

These are the glamour fish of tropical saltwater flats: skittish enough

66 The sight of a bonefish tail waving slowly above the surface of the shallow water where he customarily feeds does all kinds of things to you. You shiver and shake and tingle all over and your mouth goes dry. It is one of the great moments of all fishing experience. 99

— Joe Brooks (1950)

fussy enough to require several fly changes before you finally hit the fly du jour. And when hooked, they will accelerate almost instantly to nearly 30 miles an hour, putting your reel to the ultimate high-speed test in runs of 100-200 yards or more.

When hooked, the sleek bonefish accelerates instantly to 30 miles an hour, testing the mettle of tackle and angler alike. Bonefish range in size from 14 pounds to (more typically) 4 to 6 pounds. Yucatan bonefish, like this one taken off Boca Paila, tend to be even smaller: 1 to 3 pounds.

to require a careful stalk but sufficiently unwary to make careful stalking possible. They take small, shrimplike flies readily, but can be Average bonefish size varies widely according to region, with some of the biggest found within sight of the

---

## T E C H N I Q U E   T I P
### SPOTTING FISH

There's a real knack to this, and it'll take you a day or two on the flats before you start spotting fish with any regularity. If the sun is out, look for shadows moving along the bottom, which are often easier to see than the fish that's casting the shadow in the first place. Some things, such as fish tails waving above the surface, are more obvious. Small puffs of mud hanging in the water above the bottom are freshly made and a sign of fish very nearby. If you spot a stingray schmoozing along the bottom, look behind it. Bonefish often follow rays to catch whatever small shrimp are stirred up by the ray's passage. Reading the water's surface can help, too. A small area of water where the surface ripple is somehow different than the surrounding area can betray a school of bonefish underneath. Practice makes perfect. You'll learn by putting in your time on the water, and that sure beats going to work.

ever, and numerous schools of more than 100 fish each were common on the last Mexican flats I visited. In that particular case, I quit fishing at noon — simply tired out from hooking and playing bonefish in paradise.

Bonefish — like trout — are wary enough to require skillful stalking, yet can be approached to within fly-casting range. They take small, shrimplike flies like the BONEFISH SPECIAL (below).

## OTHER TARGETS

Other popular southern-saltwater, fly rod fish include tarpon, snook, barracuda, spotted sea trout, ladyfish, jacks, permit, and many more — even sharks that will readily take a big streamer cast with a wire leader close to their eye to ensure the fish sees the fly in the first place. The saltwater references I've highlighted in Sources & Resources detail all of these fish to some degree. I'm using this chapter to highlight solely redfish and bonefish as being the most widely distributed and popular species.

Miami skyline in south Florida's Biscayne Bay, where fish to 14 pounds have been taken on flies. Bones of 4-6 pounds are more typical, however, in both south Florida and the Bahamas, and a 30-inch 10-pounder is a monster anywhere. Yucatan bonefish tend to average smaller, 1 to 3 pounds typically, in destinations such as Boca Paila and Ascensión Bay south of Cancún. Bonefish are most plentiful here, how-

The barracuda is just one of many other saltwater fish — including spotted sea trout, permit, and even sharks — that can be taken on a fly using many of the tactics that apply to redfish and bonefish. Fly Pattern: ANDERSON'S McCRAB.

But keep in mind that many of the tactics we're about to cover apply to other shallow-water species as well.

## SEASONS

Spring and fall are the best months in the general area between south Florida, Texas, and Central America. In all of these areas, midwinter cold snaps can slow the fishing, keeping bonefish off the flats for example. These weather events are unpredictable, and predictability is important when you're trying to book a trip months in advance. Summer is also a good time, although most people don't think of southern-saltwater fly fishing in July. But I've been in the summertime Bahamas when it was a pleasant 80 degrees with low humidity, while back home in Vermont the mercury was breaking 90 amid frequent thunderstorms.

## USING A GUIDE

There are some locations along Route 1 through the Florida Keys where it's possible to park near a productive-looking flat and to start looking for bonefish. The same sort of approach can be used when redfishing along the Texas Gulf Coast. But if you haven't done it before or feel the least uncertain, your best bet is to hire a guide and boat. In the long run, you'll save both time and money; you'll catch more fish, and you'll learn a great deal from the guide.

This will cost you about $350

## PICKING A GUIDE

There's no way to tell a good guide from a bad one just by reading magazine ads. Then, too, a good guide for me might not be one for you — much depends on a personality match. The best answer is to use any one of many travel agencies that specialize in fishing trips. Happy customers are the backbone of their business. Describe your needs and skills honestly and precisely, and they'll find you a good match. This won't cost you any more money than doing things on your own, while giving more assurance of best results. Several such agencies are listed in Sources & Resources at the back of the book.

for an 8-hour fishing day in south-coastal waters; perhaps a little less and possibly a little more. Both guides and specialized fly-fishing travel services can be located through the advertisements in any of the popular fly-fishing magazines (see Sources & Resources). The special shallow-draft "flats" skiff in which you'll be fishing cost your guide somewhere around $30,000 with motor and trailer, plus he has to pay other expenses and support a

you've learned, but don't forget that the learning itself should come first.

## ON THE FLATS
### Starting Out

For the rest of this chapter, we'll walk through your first Florida Keys bone-fishing trip, the kind of trip with which most first-timers start. (Gulf Coast redfishing is in many respects similar.) You will have booked your guide by telephone several months in advance, knowing (because I've just told you) that spring and fall are prime times and that winter is some-times too cold even in Florida for successful bonefishing. After settling on a deposit, the guide will likely have asked about

On your first day or two out on the flats, you'll be relying on your guide to spot fish for you, but before long you'll recognize the signs. Polarized sun-glasses are a must, both to improve visibility and prevent eye fatigue.

your skill level, which will help him decide

family from what occasional bad weather makes into a part-time job. There are no rich guides (no matter what they charge) and the education you'll get is more than worth it. Eventually you may want to strike out on your own based on what

where and how you'll fish when the day finally arrives. Be honest when describing your skills; exaggerating here — as many do — may get you into a situation you can't handle.

He may also ask about tackle; some clients prefer their own while

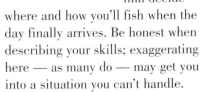

An angler crouches catlike to reduce his visibility as he retrieves line on the bonefish flats, Grassy Cays, Bahamas. Stalking bonefish on such flats is one of the great adventures of saltwater fly fishing. Just be sure to wear a hat and cover every inch of exposed skin with sunblock.

## WADING THE FLATS

This usually means wading wet in shallow water; hopefully, on a hard, sand bottom. I wear light cotton trousers for this that are comfortable and dry quickly. Some prefer shorts, but risk sunburned legs. Light socks and old sneakers will protect your feet against sharp coral and spiny things like small sea urchins. Make sure your sneakers fit tightly enough to not pull off in occasional muddy spots; and never — not ever — wade barefoot.

Many flats, notably in the Bahamas and Mexico, are hard-bottomed, where wading is like walking on a sidewalk. Others are muck, some treacherously so. More than one regular in south Florida's Biscayne Bay has used snowshoes in wading there as a means of traversing soft flats. If exploring on your own, be tentative at first, going only as far as the bottom remains hard. If you encounter a soft flat, stay off it. You may otherwise get stuck with no help in sight.

"There's one!" the guide hisses. "Nine o'clock! Sixty feet! Tailing! Tailing! See it?" On your first time out, your response to the guide's excited directions will likely be frantic confusion. The next thing you know, however, you'll have a bonefish on and you won't have time to think. Fly Pattern: NIX'S EPOXY FLY.

others use the guide's. First-timers should try the guide's gear before making a substantial investment in their own tackle. For your own gear, you'll want an 8- or 9-weight, 9-foot rod with matching weight-forward floating line and 200 yards of backing set up on a smooth-running reel. Some rod companies tout their 7-weights as the "ultimate bonefish rod," but that's only true in the hands of an ultimate caster. The 8- and 9-weights handle much better in the inevitable breeze; leave the lighter 6- and 7-weights to genuine experts. A few 9-foot leaders tapered to 10-pound-test and a box of bonefish flies (see Chapter 14) complete the basic gear, but don't forget your jacket, hat, sunblock, clippers, insect repellent, spare tippet material, pliers, camera, and polarized sunglasses — all of which pack in the small duffel bag you'll take on board.

## First Time on Board

So you fly to Miami, rent a car, and drive about an hour south to a motel near Key Largo, thinking alternately of bonefish and the old Bogart movie. At 8 a.m. or thereabouts on the next morning, you meet your guide at the marina a few miles south. He stows your gear on board a long, slim-looking boat with a huge outboard motor on the back, and will probably put your rod in an interior rack so it won't bounce around. You'll sit in a comfortable seat toward the bow, just in front of the skipper's console. Put on your jacket and sunglasses before you sit. When you hear the motor start, grab your hat and hold it firmly. These boats are *fast* — sometimes running at 40 to 50 miles an hour or even more, and there's no windshield in front of you to break the breeze. People lose lots of hats this way.

## Basic Procedure

You'll stop soon — a little relieved — out on the flats, probably for a practice session as the skipper explains the drill. Take your fully rigged rod and stand on the open casting deck at the bow. Following instructions, strip enough line off the reel to make the longest cast of which you're capable; say, 60 feet. Having cast, then strip in line, allowing the line to fall in large, loose coils on the deck in front of your feet. Don't step or stand on the line!

## GEAR TALK

### SALTWATER FLY REELS

There's one real bargain in this field, and that's the venerable Model 1498 Pfleuger Medalist reel, which you can still buy for less than $50. This is big enough and strong enough to take everything a big bonefish can dish out. But after several fish, the reel may heat up too much and start to sound creaky, at which point you'll wish you had something better. Possibilities range from $100 or so on up to about $900 or even more. I checked my own reel cabinet and figured the average price of six saltwater reels there at $450. Now I'm sorry I looked!

All premium saltwater reels function well; I'm not aware of a really bad one. There are two types. Anti-reverse reels are convenient because the handle remains stationary while the spool revolves as the fish takes line. This means a spinning handle won't whack your knuckles. So-called direct-drive reels don't have this feature, but are stronger and tougher in playing really big fish. Both styles feature large, durable drag systems usually similar in design to automotive clutches. In any case, remember to gently rinse your reel in fresh water after fishing to prevent corrosion.

## Casting

Leave about 25 feet of line plus leader and fly extending beyond the top rod guide, grab that line with your left hand, then work your hand down so you're holding just the fly

Bonefish bound: A selection of bonefish flies and tackle. The speed with which hooked bonefish run puts enormous strain on the reel, and it's easy to spend $450 on a model that can take the punishment.

extending the line to the target. If — like many trout fishermen — you persist in making half a dozen back-and-forth false casts before delivery, the bonefish will be long gone. Your skipper may have you try this a few times to make sure you've got the hang of it before you actually start fishing.

## Fishing, at Last

When you're ready and the location is right, the skipper will likely climb onto a small platform built above the outboard motor at the stern, from which he'll slowly push the boat with a long pole along the shallow

with your thumb and index finger on the hook bend *behind* the hookpoint. The line and leader trail in a large curve between your left hand and the rod tip. This is your "ready" position. When you need to quickly cast to a fish, flip the line in the air and let go the fly simultaneously, make one strong backcast, then a forward cast

flat. Ideally, the sun will be at your back to make spotting fish easiest. The breeze will be at your back, too, for easiest casting. Sometimes this combination actually happens; at other times things are just that much more difficult.

It's like being in a mystical aquarium as small rays, sharks, and

Tarpon, which range from Cape Hatteras to Brazil, can weigh 200 pounds and tow a boat for miles. The hard-mouthed, powerful fish "tail walk," flinging their entire bodies clear of the water and shaking their heads in a usually successful effort to throw hooks. Landing even a "baby" tarpon of 20 pounds is a lifetime dream fulfilled for saltwater fly fishermen.

other fish appear suddenly within your sight range and waggle briefly by your magic carpet. The reverie of sun and gently slapping water is quietly wonderful and suddenly broken.

"There's one!" the guide hisses, jamming the pole into the mud, stopping the boat short and nearly tipping you off the front. "Nine o'clock! Sixty feet!"

Think fast, my friend. Now let's see. Twelve o'clock is straight ahead, so nine o'clock must be off there to the left somewhere. Sixty feet, he said. You look and see nothing.

"Tailing! Tailing! See it? See it?" There's a little silver flash that looks almost like a wave and the sudden appearance of a small mud cloud in the same spot. The mud?

"Yes! Right there! The mud! Cast three feet to the left of the mud! He's moving left! Now! Now!"

So you cast in a hurry and the fly line settles more or less pointed toward the mud and you never realized it all happened this fast and your personal cool has erupted in heartbeats that sound like thunder. Rod tip down, line under your right index finger — some rules never change. Short strips. Four inches. Strip. Strip.

"Coming! He's turned and he's coming! Strip! Strip! Strip!" The guide calls the cadence.

Out beyond the end of the fly line, out where the fly should be, is a pale gray shape moving slowly toward you. So that's what they look like! On the next strip the line feels tighter somehow....

"Hit him! Raise your rod! Watch out for your slack line! There he goes! Lookit'm! Lookit'm go!'"

## Playing Fish

In the second or two you used to check the slack line at your feet, that slack has gone slapping up against the rod butt. The line is tight, the reel whirring, and that big wake speeding off in the distance — unbelievable distance — is your fish.

Eventually the fish will stop, and then circle as you slowly retrieve line on the reel. There will be a second run most likely, shorter than the first, and more circles until the fish is at the boat and netted. The guide will remove the fly, then probably give you the bonefish to hold briefly — one hand on the tail, the other supporting its body.

"Six pounds," the guide says, taking a photo. The fish feels cool in your hands, its body very hard with muscle. A lovely silver fish tinted with green waves along its back that you release gently into silver water where it fades and disappears in tints of green.

A shadow. A memory. An oh-my-God-I-really-did-it bonefish.

### KEEP IN MIND

- Use a guide for your first attempts; the education is worth it.
- Understand the kind of casting required. Practice at home!
- Never — but never — go out on the flats without wearing sunblock. The sun is brutal.
- Spring and fall are the best times.
- Use a specialized travel agent; happy fishermen are their business.

# 13
# FLY TYING

One of our friends was up from the city a few weeks ago, an older woman who had never done any fly fishing but thought it sounded interesting. She was incredulous when I said she could not only catch a trout, but also make the fly she'd be using in the first place. Fly tying, I explained, has a lot of mystique and sounds very arcane, but is really very simple. So I poured us some coffee, opened a box of cookies, and set up a fly-tying vise on the kitchen table.

A turn here. A twist there. And soon her unfamiliar fingers had produced a small and very fishable Hare's Ear nymph. This fly would win no prizes at the local trout club, but it would, I assured her, catch fish no matter how scruffy it looked. Later that afternoon, I loaned her some waders and we headed for the neighborhood stream. We tied on her nymph and used the no-cast fishing method I describe on page 84. She took two trout in about half an hour of slowly working the stream—a small brookie and an acrobatic 10-inch rainbow. Some days later when we next spoke by phone, I heard all about the kind of waders she was going to get, what rod, and where she planned to fish that weekend.

Don't be put off by the supposed complexity of fly tying. Everyone starts somewhere, and even your first attempts can be successful in taking fish as long as you've picked the right pattern and size for your particular fishing.

## FLY-TYING KITS

Most major retailers and mail-order fly-fishing suppliers offer these kits, which are the best way to start. This way you're assured of having all the right ingredients for a series of different flies with proven success. The quality of the tools included with better kits is generally high. And most of the better kits also include an excellent instruction book developed through many years of trial and error in teaching beginners.

Just remember that you'll get what you pay for. Most kits selling for something like $29.95 are worthless, assembled from poor-quality tying materials and tools that are simply junk. A first-rate kit from a reputable supplier will start at about $135 and offers tools suited to a lifetime of use. Higher prices usually include even better tools, a better instruction book, and more materials. Most kits are designed around trout flies, but there are also specialized kits for bass flies and for saltwater.

## VIDEOS

Beyond kits themselves, the next most helpful thing will be a fly-tying videotape. There are a great many of these, most of which offer superb close-up photography that you can play and replay, stopping for study as needed. They are an extremely effective and simple way to learn specific techniques, such as putting the wings on a dry fly or adding legs to a bass bug.

## FLY-TYING TOOLS

VISE: Basically a simple clamp that uses a short lever to pull opposing jaws against the bend of a hook, holding the hook firmly as you work. They range from the inexpensive, venerable, and still-standard Thompson Model A at about $30 up to sculpture-like, precision-machined models costing several hundred dollars. Most clamp to a tabletop; some have weighted, free-standing bases that are more convenient.

BOBBIN: Holds and helps to control your tying thread. The thread spool fits between opposing arms that can be bent to adjust thread tension. The arms are attached to a fine-diameter tube through which your thread passes and that allows precise placement of thread wraps on the fly.

BOBBIN CLEANER/THREADER: The cleaner part is a simple rod used to push dirt and debris free from the bobbin tube. The threader is a fine wire loop like a needle threader. Pass it through the bobbin tube, put

Fly-tying feathers, clockwise from lower left: red rooster saddle, dark cream rooster saddle, premium grizzly dry-fly rooster neck (in front of spools of thread and tinsel), brown hen neck, blue dun (gray) hen neck, white turkey quill, mallard quill, cream rooster neck, wood-duck flank feathers, black rooster saddle, and brown hen neck (center).

yours don't have sharp edges on the jaws, which will cut the feather itself.

BODKIN: Simply a needle useful in untangling things, clearing hook eyes, and applying small drops of head cement or glue. Make one by sticking a sewing needle into the eraser on the end of a pencil.

There are lots of other specialty fly-tying tools, but only the foregoing are essential.

thread through the wire loop, then pull the thread back out through the bobbin tube.

SCISSORS: Fine points are helpful, as is sharpness. Some specialty fly-tying scissors may cost as much as $75 a pair; mine are small sewing scissors that cost $7 at the local department store.

HACKLE PLIERS: A simple, small clamp to hold the end of a hackle feather when winding that feather around a hook. There are many inexpensive designs; just make sure

## MATERIALS

Most important: Keep your furs and feathers in *sealed* Ziploc bags together with some moth crystals (paradichlorobenzene) to prevent infestations of dermestid beetle larvae, which will literally eat up your collection if they get out of control.

THREAD: Traditionalists still use hard-to-find silk, but today's standard

wound on the hook shank to produce a shaped body. DUBBING WAX: A tacky fly-tying wax that comes in a lipstick-like tube. Used to coat thread, making it tacky to accept the application of loose fur. HEAD CEMENT: A variety of cements and lacquers used to coat the thread wraps at various tying stages, as well as the fly head when done. There

This premium fly-tying kit sells for just under $200. It includes a quality vise (center), Dick Talleur's *Fly Tyer's Primer*, and a complement of the furs, feathers, hooks, and other materials you'll need to get started. Tools include: a bobbin (just below the vise jaws, loaded with a spool of black thread), hackle pliers (right of the bobbin), a whip finisher (left of the blue-handled scissors), and a bodkin (below the whip finisher).

is nylon. The most common is what's called "6/0 nylon prewaxed," which conforms to an archaic "0" sizing system and in this case corresponds to medium-fine. "Prewaxed" means the thread has a light coating of tacky wax that helps to keep it from slipping and sliding around on the hook. Available in a rainbow of colors, of which black, brown, red, olive, white, and yellow are basic. BODY MATERIALS: Things like wool yarns and fuzzy chenille in various colors and diameters that can be

are many specialty fly-tying brands. Plain spar varnish from the hardware store also works well, as does "Jane's Hard-As-Nails" nail polish from your local drugstore. TINSEL: Formerly of metal, now of a plastic called Mylar and often silver on one side and gold on the other. Of assorted widths and spooled like thread. Used to add flash to a fly.

## Feathers

Many complex choices, but here are the basics:

HACKLE: Feathers from the neck area of a chicken, often sold on the skin, hence the name "neck." Often bred expressly for fly tying, premium rooster necks can cost $75 or more. These are used primarily for dry flies. (Save money by buying lower grades and/or half necks, which are more than ample.) Hen necks have shorter, softer hackle used for wets and nymphs. Freshwater and salt-water streamers use long, fluttery "saddle" hackles, which come from the middle rear or saddle of the bird's back.

QUILLS: The primary and secondary flight feathers of a variety of birds, including ducks, geese, and turkeys, sections of which are often used as fly wings. The cinnamon-mottled secondary wing quills of brown turkeys, for example, are used for Muddler Minnow wings.

BODY PLUMAGE: Shorter soft feathers from a variety of birds, most commonly used as hackle in wets and nymphs. Also used for winging some flies; the wings of a Light Cahill dry are made from a male wood-duck flank feather, for example.

MARABOU: Originally from a kind of stork; now taken from domestic turkeys. These are long-fibered, soft fluffy feathers, fibers from which are bunched to make very wiggly streamer wings.

## Furs

BUCKTAILS: Tails from (most commonly) white-tailed deer that have extremely long-fibered hair, as much as 6 inches or more. Used primarily for the wings on fresh-water and saltwater streamers. Other kinds of tails (for example, calf) are widely available, have shorter fibers, and are most useful for smaller flies.

DUBBING FURS: Soft, short-fibered furs that are clipped, then spun around waxed thread, making a soft fur yarn that's then wound for a fly body. Beaver and rabbit are two types that are soft, easily worked, and available in a variety of dyed colors.

DEERHAIR: Patches of hide with hair attached from the body area of (commonly) white-tailed deer. These hairs are hollow, and can be packed and spun around a hook shank, then trimmed to make a Muddler Minnow head or a deerhair bass bug. Elk, antelope, and caribou hairs are also used for the same purpose.

## HERE, KITTY

Those are a very few basics, most of which will be contained in your kit or starter collection. The possibilities are limited only by your imagination, but a word of caution. When you're tying quietly and start looking at your dog or cat in a speculative way, forget it. The fur from neither one works as well as more standard materials.

## TYING A GOLD-RIBBED HARE'S EAR NYMPH

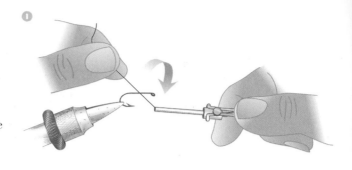

**1** Clamp hook in vise as shown. Use left hand to hold free end of thread at an angle across and against the back of the hook shank. Right hand holds thread bobbin.

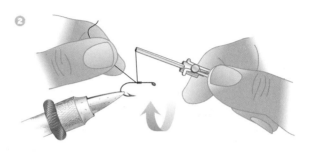

**2** Wind thread with right hand away from your body and around the hook, securing thread to shank. After about ten turns, trim excess free end of thread.

**3** Measure three or four wood-duck flank-feather fibers for tails by holding them along the hook. Tails should be about one shank-length long.

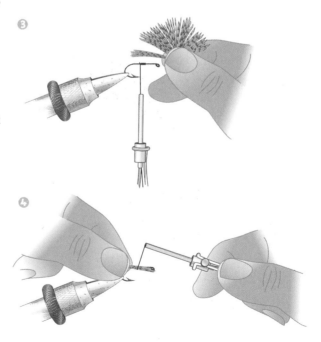

**4** Start winding thread clockwise as you hold fiber butts against near side of hook. Thread rotation will roll the fiber butts properly to the top of hook shank.

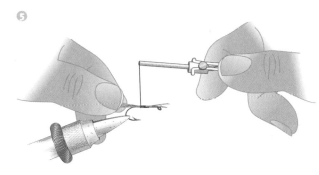

**❺** Wind thread to rear while holding fibers in position with left hand.

**❻** Raise and spread the tail fibers with one thread turn under and behind them. Then wind thread back to middle of shank and fasten fine, oval-gold-tinsel ribbing.

**❼** Coat thread with tacky dubbing wax. Don't use too much.

**❽** Pluck — don't cut — some soft fur from a mottled-brown hare's mask. Use right index finger to hold fur gently against waxed thread.

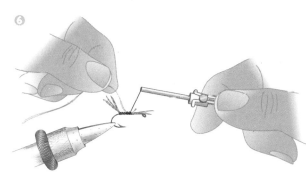

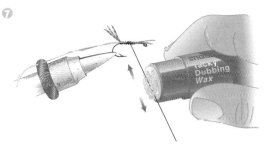

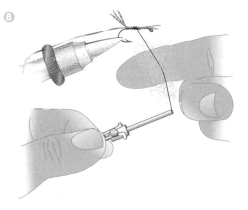

**❾** Pinch fur between thumb and index finger and use a rolling motion to spin fur into a loose yarn around the thread. Roll in one direction only; not back and forth.

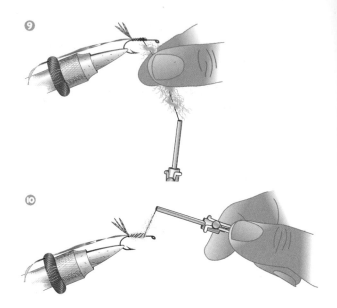

**❿** Wind fur yarn in a neatly tapered shape over rear two-thirds of shank, also binding tinsel to rear of hook.

**⓫** A one-eighth-inch wide section of gray, mallard-wing quill for nymph's wingcase.

**⓬** As with tails, hold quill section at hook's side when you start winding to roll the quill section with thread to the top of the hook.

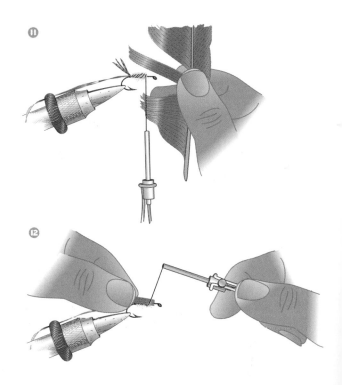

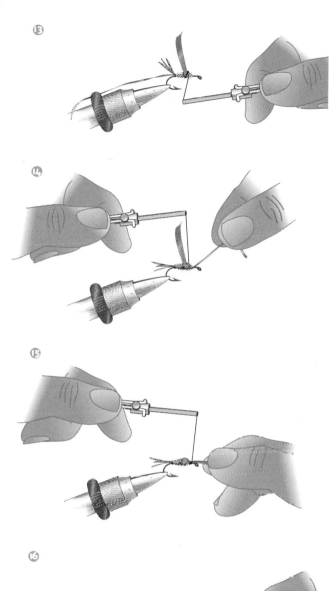

⑬ Add more fur dubbing forward of the tied-in quill section.

⑭ Wind gold ribbing forward with three open turns behind wingcase and two in front. Tie off with thread and trim excess.

⑮ Pull the wingcase tightly down and over the hook eye with your right hand, securing with thread. Be sure you've left plenty of room for a small, neat head. Trim excess quill.

⑯ Complete the fly with a whip-finish knot. Tie in a short loop of thread at the fly's head, and use your left index finger to push against the rear of the fly to hold everything together while you complete the next step.

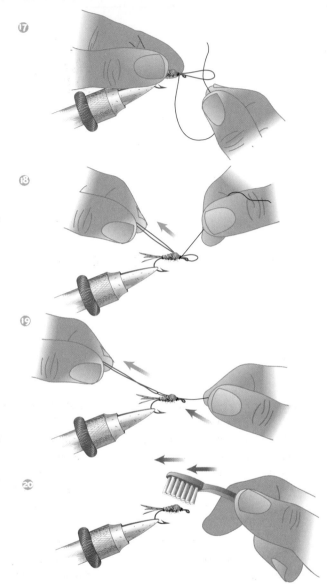

⑰ Pull a few inches of thread from the bobbin, cut it and then insert free end through loop.

⑱ Grab the free thread end as it comes through the loop with your right hand and maintain tension. Pull on the end of the thread loop with your left hand.

⑲ This action pulls the tying thread back under a series of its own wraps, creating a durable knot. Trim excess. Add a small drop of nail polish or head cement to the thread wraps to make the fly even more durable.

⑳ Brush the fur body with rearward strokes, using a small toothbrush. This roughens the body, making it more life-like in the water.

## KEEP IN MIND

- Make your life easy; start with a good fly-tying kit.
- Fly-tying videos are excellent for learning techniques.
- Protect your tying materials in sealed bags with moth crystals.
- You *can* do this — really; I promise!

# FAVORITE FLIES

A fly pattern is a kind of recipe that specifies tying materials and style for a particular fly. There are tens of thousands of different fly patterns, some of which are distinctive and vital in one or more types of fly fishing while others are just bit players. The reason for this extravagant and often confusing largesse goes back to the very nature of fly patterns themselves.

Nelson Bryant, who for many years wrote a delightfully erudite outdoor column for the *New York Times*, once suggested that the concept of fly pattern evolved centuries ago as a simple means of communication—one that answered the inevitable

angler's question: "Whad'ja catch 'em on?" That idea is both simple and profound, meaning that answering "a Royal Coachman wet" is much more specific than saying "a little fly with a white wing."

Slight changes can tell you even more. When yellow is substituted for the red-banded middle of our Royal Coachman, it becomes a California Coachman. Omit the band entirely and substitute a gray wing, and the fly becomes a Leadwing Coachman. And so on.

Following are specific notes on 27 different flies, covering the gamut from trout to saltwater. All are widely used nationally, and all are commer

If you had to pick just one fly with which to fish for trout, bass, and panfish, it would be the Muddler Minnow (see page 178), a versatile streamer fly invented in the 1930s that, depending on the size you select, will nicely pass for all manner of small baitfish, a grasshopper, or a large nymph.

cially available. Eventually, you'll probably wind up with many more than what I've included here, but these standards can get you started.

## TROUT AND PANFISH FLIES

ADAMS: The most popular all-around trout dry fly. An old Michigan pattern, it's generally representative of small, drab mayflies and caddis-flies. Carry an assortment of sizes from 12 down to 20, matching your selection to the size of the hatching flies of the moment.

LIGHT CAHILL: A traditional Catskill trout dry fly, and a specific imitation of a large (#12-#14) cream-colored mayfly common to Catskill rivers in early June. This fly answers the need for a light-colored pattern as counterpoint to the Adams, which is dark. Useful sizes: 12-18.

PARACHUTE BLUE-WINGED OLIVE: Mayflies of this color scheme (dark olive-green body/slate wing) are common nationwide in sizes 14 down to 26. The parachute style features horizontal hackle, placing the fly flat on the surface, and is more specifically representative of an emerging insect.

**GRIFFITHS GNAT:** A terrific dry in small sizes from 18 down to 24; use when trout are quietly taking near-invisible minutiae at the surface. Named after George Griffiths, who founded Trout Unlimited in Michigan in 1958.

**ELK HAIR CADDIS:** A high-floating caddis dry developed by Montana fly tier Al Troth. Now basic equipment nationwide in sizes 14-20 and in colors including tan, dun (gray), and olive.

**GOLD-RIBBED HARE'S EAR NYMPH:** The great all-purpose nymph pattern; useful sizes from 10 down to 20. If you can find them, carry a few that are weighted with lead wire under the fur body for fishing deep.

**OLIVE FUR CADDIS PUPA:** Caddis swimming rapidly to the surface are in the emergent pupal stage, and their active movement often triggers slashing rises from trout. Useful sizes are 14-20. Cream and tan colors also work well at times.

**ZUG BUG:** A dark nymph and useful counterpoint to the medium-toned Hare's Ear. Specifically, an imitation of a mayfly with the Latin name *Isonychia*, but also widely useful in sizes 12 down to 18.

**LIGHT CAHILL WET:** Many trout dry flies have wet fly counterparts, and this is a favorite. Great for searching a stream with down-and-across casts; also a good panfish fly. Sizes 12-18.

**ROYAL COACHMAN WET:** An American classic wet fly, originally concocted in a nineteenth-century Vermont kitchen. Still bright and fun to use for brook trout, especially in ponds, and a super panfish fly in sizes 12-16.

**BLACK GHOST:** Now a favorite streamer for brown trout nationwide, but originally an early-1900s Maine landlocked salmon fly. Try sizes up to 4 for larger trout and down to 12 for perch and panfishes.

**GRAY GHOST:** Our most famous traditional streamer fly, first tied on July 1, 1924 by Mrs. Carrie Stevens at Upper Dam, Maine. Best for landlocked salmon and brook trout in sizes 2 down to 10.

**MUDDLER MINNOW:** The one fly to have. This streamer pattern dates back to the 1930s and is now ubiquitous. Large sizes to 1/0 for big trout. Fished dry in sizes 8-12, it's a grasshopper imitation. Fished wet in the same sizes, it's a small minnow or large nymph. Don't leave home without some.

**BLACK WOOLLY BUGGER:** The black, wiggly thing that everything loves. Fish slow and deep with lots of twitches in sizes 4 to 10, especially for rainbow trout and smallmouth bass.

## BASS FLIES

**CLOUSER MINNOW:** This streamer style features dumbbell-shaped lead eyes at the head, which makes it sink rapidly and then dart erratically when twitched. Basic equipment for smallmouth bass, but also a good all-around style in both freshwater and saltwater in sizes 4 to 10.

**HARE WATER PUP:** This rabbit-fur fly and similar styles made with long fur strips or hackle feathers undulate up and down when slowly stripped through the water. Many colors; my favorite is purple on a 1/0 hook.

**CLOUSER CRAYFISH:** Like Clouser Minnows, this fly is weighted near the hook eye to get down fast. This or any other crayfish imitation is important for smallmouth bass, but will also take stream trout — especially large browns that often feed on crayfish. Sizes 6-10.

**HAIR BUG:** Representative of a whole family of deerhair bass bugs. Make sure yours are tied on hooks with a wide gap between hook point and shank so the fly's materials don't interfere with its hooking ability. Colors and styles unlimited; hook sizes 2 or 6 common.

**POPPING BUG:** One of a generic class of hard-bodied, cupped-face poppers that will float longer than deerhair versions. Note the all-important wide hook gap. Sizes 2 (big fish),

6 (medium-size fish), and 10 (small bass and big bluegills).

## SALTWATER NORTH

**SKIPPING BUG:** The classic saltwater popper, and a favorite for both striped bass and bluefish. Experimenting with retrieve speeds is usually a key; best at dawn or dusk, poor after dark. Sizes 2 and 2/0, with the bigger version being harder to cast.

**ROGER'S SAND EEL:** One of many now-popular sand-eel imitations with the key characteristic of a long, slim profile. Useful sizes from 1/0 down to 6 for striped bass and bluefish, fished with a slow, swimming retrieve.

**POPOVIC'S SURF CANDY:** The clear epoxy-resin head is both realistic and very durable. Excellent striper fly when the bass are on smaller bait such as spearing. In even smaller sizes, also good for bonito. Sizes 1/0 to 6.

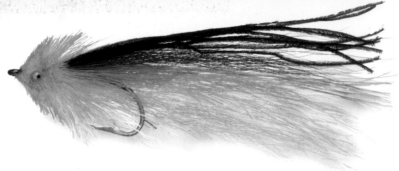

**TABORY'S SLAB FLY:** A broad-bodied streamer imitative of such baitfish as menhaden (bunker) and herring, both favored striper foods. Its shape is a distinct counterpoint to a slim sand eel, for example, and that difference can be important. Sizes 2/0 and 4/0.

## SALTWATER SOUTH

**ANDERSON'S MCCRAB:** Tied especially for permit on tropical flats, but also an effective bonefish fly that's good, too, for striped bass that often feed on crabs in northern waters. Sizes 1/0 and 2.

**BONEFISH SPECIAL:** Excellent all-around bonefish fly with a compar-

atively slow sinking rate. That means it's especially adapted to very shallow water. Good in sizes 4 down to 8.

**CRAZY CHARLIE:** Bead-chain eyes weight this bonefish fly at the head, which means it sinks fairly fast and offers a more rapid up-and-down jigging action than other styles when retrieved. Many colors; I like tan, gray, or white. Sizes 4 to 8.

**NIX'S EPOXY FLY:** One of many fast-sinking bonefish flies with epoxy-resin heads designed to look like small shrimp. Extremely durable and realistic in sizes 4-8.

# SOURCES & RESOURCES

Now that this book has whetted your fly-fishing interest and gotten you started with basic equipment and skills, you'll want to learn even more. The most obvious next step is to go fishing, where time spent on the water with an open, inquisitive mind often proves to be the best instructor. Beyond fishing itself, sources of more information are legion, each potentially adding to a fund of knowledge that will continue to grow throughout your fishing life.

The best place to start, other than a fly-fishing school (see p. 182), is with any one of the several specialized fly-fishing magazines. In addition to informative articles, all of these magazines include numerous advertisements from a variety of fly-fishing businesses. Write for — and read — the mail-order catalogs, which provide a wealth of information in addition to offering diverse gear.

## ASSOCIATIONS & ORGANIZATIONS

If you are looking for company, for clubs, or simply for information, call any of these organizations. They are all eager to promote their interests and yours. Often they will have lists of local groups or individuals that you can contact.

### AMERICAN MUSEUM OF FLY FISHING

P.O. Box 42
Manchester, VT 05254
802-362-3300; fax 802-362-3308
*Open all year; exhibits by leading wildlife artists; traveling exhibit called "Angler's All." Publishes quarterly magazine, "American Fly Fisher," for members.*

### AMERICAN RIVERS

(formerly American Rivers Conservation Council)
801 Pennsylvania Avenue, SE, Suite 400
Washington, D.C. 20003
202-547-6900
*A public interest organization working for river protection. Several publications.*

### FEDERATION OF FLY FISHERS

P.O. Box 1595
Bozeman, MT 59771
406-585-7592, 800-618-0808;
fax 406-585-7596
E-mail: *74504.2605@compuserve.com*; Home page:
*http://www.wsa.com/ool/fff.html
Education and conservation organization with 200 affiliated clubs; five times a year publishes "The Flyfisher." Clubs offer educational programs, Internet services, published materials and programs for children.*

## TROUT UNLIMITED
1500 Wilson Boulevard,
Suite 310
Arlington, VA 22209
703-284-9411; fax 703-284-9400
*Perhaps the leading national conservation organization focusing on trout and salmon and their environments, dedicated to preserving, protecting, and restoring cold water fisheries and their watersheds. 450 chapters nationwide, offering monthly meetings, newsletter, and clinics in conservation and angling.*

## FLY-FISHING SCHOOLS
By far the best way to get started, fly-fishing workshops are offered by many local dealers and local chapters of Trout Unlimited or the Federation of Fly Fishers. Some are run by fishing-tackle companies, others by well-known casting teachers such as Joan Wulff and Mel Krieger. Write for brochures and reservation information.

### L.L. BEAN FLY-FISHING SCHOOLS
Tom Ackerman
Freeport, ME 04033
800-341-4341, x6666
Home page:
*http://www.llbean.com/odp/fish/index.html*
*2-6-day classes in both fly tying and fresh and saltwater fishing, mainly during the summer on the East Coast Their 3-day introductory course is a very popular offering.*

### MEL KRIEGER SCHOOL OF FLY-FISHING
790 27th Avenue
San Francisco, CA 94121
415-752-0192; fax 415-752-0804
*Offers 2-5-day workshops all over the country.*

### ORVIS FISHING SCHOOLS
Manchester, VT 05254
800-235-9763; fax 540-343-7053
in Canada: 800-541-3541
Home page: *http://www.alloutdoors.com/orvis/Schools/SunNeverSets.html*
*Guide services and year-round schools in Florida, Massachusetts,*

*Colorado, New York, and Vermont. All staff trained to respond to queries (call the number above) on gear and technique.*

### WULFF SCHOOL OF FLY FISHING
HCR 1, Box 70
Lew Beach, NY 12758
914-439-4060
*Workshops offered weekends throughout the spring in New York's Catskill region, long famous for its trout streams.*

## TRAVEL
There are thousands of worthwhile fly-fishing destinations worldwide, ranging from popular rivers in the Rockies and West to such exotic targets as African tigerfish, Austrian grayling, and the famous trout fishing in Argentina, Chile, and New Zealand. Popular locations may be served by dozens of local outfitters — the Florida Keys is one example — which makes long-distance choices almost impossible for the novice. The best answer is to use any one of several specialized fishing travel agents. Happy customers are their business, and bookings cost no more than doing it yourself because the agency's commission is paid by the lodge or outfitter. Most such agents offer catalogs, for which you should write. Possibilities include:

### ANGLER ADVENTURES
Box 872
Old Lyme, CT 06371
800-628-1447

### BOB MARRIOTT'S FLYFISHING STORE
2700 West Orangethorpe
Fullerton, CA 92633
714-525-1827; fax 714-525-5783

### FISHING INTERNATIONAL
Box 2132
Santa Rosa, CA 95405
800-950-4242; fax 707-539-1320

### THE FLY SHOP
4140 Churn Creek Road
Reading, CA 96002
800-669-3474; fax 916-222-3572

### FRONTIERS INTERNATIONAL
Box 161
Wexford, PA 15090
800-245-1950

## MAGAZINES
The established fishing magazines can both thrill and lend assurance to novices. They are chock full of techniques, recommendations, and usually ample back sections with advertisements for fishing schools, guides, outfitters, travel agents, and gear.

### AMERICAN ANGLER
Abenaki Publishers, Inc.
Box 4100
Bennington, VT 05201-4100
802-447-1518; fax 802-447-2471

### FIELD & STREAM
Times Mirror Magazines, Inc.
2 Park Avenue,
New York, NY 10016
212-779-5000; fax 212-725-3836

### FLY FISHERMAN
Cowles Magazines, Inc.
Box 8200
Harrisburg, PA 17105
717-657-9555; fax 717-657-9526

### FLY ROD & REEL
Down East Enterprise, Inc.
Box 679
Camden, ME 04843
207-594-9544; fax 207-594-7215

### FLYFISHER
Federation of Fly Fishers
Box 722
Sandpoint, ID 83864
208-263-3573

### FLYFISHING
Frank Amato Publications
Box 82112
Portland, OR 97282
503-653-8151; fax 503-653-2766

### OUTDOOR LIFE
Times Mirror Magazines, Inc.
2 Park Avenue
New York, NY 10016
Subscribe to: Box 54733
Boulder, CO 80322
800-365-1580

## SPORTS AFIELD
Hearst Magazines
250 West 55th Street
New York, NY 10019
Subscribe to: Box 7166
Read Oak, IA 51591
212-649-4000

## FISHING ON THE INTERNET
Trailside® Online has been established to provide up-to-date news and views on all the topics covered in this book as well as the other Trailside Guides and all the outdoor activities enjoyed by Trailside viewers and readers worldwide. Visit us at *http://www.trailside.com* for in-depth information and entertainment. The Trailside internet site also includes valuable pointers and links to other sites on fly-fishing.

Fishing sites on the World Wide Web are proliferating like schools of bluegills. There are far too many to list here, but use an Internet search tool or index like Yahoo to search for "fishing" or "fly fishing," and you'll get a listing of several dozen sites. We can get you started with a couple of sites that have a good selection of pointers:

*http://www.flyfield.com/trib2.htm*
*http://www.lightlink.com/ephemera/interest.html*
*http://www.yahoo.com.recreation*

Check out some great cooperative Internet pages called "The AP Volunteers Section" — folk who provide information on specific waters that they fish:

*http://www.peak.org/~robertr/contacts.htm*

Remember that you can join or read about the Federation of Fly Fishers in their excellent pages: *http://www.wsa.com/ool/fff.html*

Also on the Internet are Usenet newsgroups, including rec.outdoors.fishing.fly, rec.outdoors. fishing, rec.outdoors.fishing.saltwater, and alt.fishing. All of these sometimes contain valuable fly-fishing tips.

## BOOKS
The most prolific publisher of fly-fishing books has long been Nick Lyons in New York City. To get a complete catalog from which you may order, write:

### LYONS & BURFORD PUBLISHERS
31 West 21st Street
New York, NY 10010
212-620-9580;
fax 212-929-1836

### GENERAL
*American Fly Fishing: A History,* Paul Schullery. 1992. $35.00. Lyons & Burford.

*Fly-Fishing With Children: A Guide for Parents,* Philip Brunquell. 1995. $14.00. Countryman Press.

*The New American Trout Fishing,* John Merwin. 1994. $30.00. Macmillan.
*The only overview of trout fishing in America currently in print, this book is the logical next step for beginners eager to take to trout streams.*

*Western Fly Fishing Guide,* Dave Hughes. 1987. $5.95. Frank Amato Publications.

### FLY CASTING
*Fly Fishing: Simple to Sophisticated,* Al Kyte. 1987. $13.95. Human Kinetics.

*Joan Wulff's Fly Casting Technique,* Joan Wulff. 1991. $19.95. Lyons & Burford.

### FLY FISHING FOR WOMEN
*A Different Angle: Fly Fishing Stories by Women,* Holly Morris, ed. 1996. $12.00.

*Joan Wulff's Fly Fishing: Expert Advice from a Woman's Perspective,* Joan Wulff. 1991. $19.95. Stackpole.

*Little Rivers: Tales of a Woman Angler,* Margot Page. 1996. $9.00. Avon.

### FLY TYING
*The Book of Fly Patterns,* Eric Leiser. 1987. $49.50. Knopf.

*The Complete Book of Fly Tying,* Eric Leiser. 1977. $27.50. Knopf.

*Designing Trout Flies,* Gary Borger. 1991. $19.95. Tomorrow River Press.

*John Merwin's Fly Tying Guide,* John Merwin. 1990. $10.95. Viking.

*Practical Fishing Knots II,* Mark Sosin and Lefty Kreh. 1991. $10.95. Lyons & Burford.

*Saltwater Fly Tying,* Frank Wentink. 1994. $22.95. Lyons & Burford.

### SALTWATER
*Fly Fishing for Bonefish,* Dick Brown. 1993. $35.00. Lyons & Burford.

*Fly Fishing in Saltwater,* Lefty Kreh. 1988. $24.95. Lyons & Burford.

*Fly Fishing the Tidewaters,* Tom Earnhardt. 1995. $40.00. Lyons & Burford.

*Inshore Fly Fishing,* Lou Tabory. 1993. $32.95. Lyons & Burford.

*Practical Saltwater Fly Fishing,* Mark Sosin. 1989. $19.95. Lyons & Burford.

*Tabory's Guide to Saltwater Baits and Their Imitations,* Lou Tabory. 1995. $16.95. Lyons & Burford.

### TROUT-STREAM INSECTS
*Caddisflies.* Gary LaFontaine. 1979. $35.00. Lyons & Burford.

*Hatches II,* Al Caucci and Bob Nastasi. 1990. $37.95. Lyons & Burford.

*Matching the Hatch*, Ernest Schwiebert. 1982. $11.95. Stoeger Pub. (reprint of 1955 Macmillan edition).

*Nymph Fishing for Larger Trout*, Charles Brooks. 1988. $14.95. Lyons & Burford.

*Nymphing: A Basic Book*, Gary Borger. 1979. $16.95. Stackpole. *Nymphs*, Ernest Schwiebert. 1973. Winchester Press. Out of print.

*Trout Stream Insects: an Orvis Streamside Guide*, Dick Pobst 1989. $16.95. Lyons & Burford.

## TROUT TACTICS
*Fly Fishing Small Streams*, John Gierach. 1989. $14.95. Stackpole Books.

*Fly-Fishing Strategy*, Doug Swisher and Carl Richards. 1988. $17.95. Lyons & Burford.

*Micropatterns: Tying & Fishing the Small Fly*, Darrell Martin. 1994. $40.00. Lyons & Burford.

*Nymph Fishing*, Dave Hughes. 1995. $15.95. Frank Amato Publications.

*Slack Line Strategies for Fly Fishing*, John Judy. 1994. $19.95. Stackpole Books.

*Steelhead Fly Fishing*, Trey Combs. 1991. $40.00. Lyons & Burford (Original paperback may be available at $19.95.)

*Stonefly and Caddis Fly-Fishing*, L. Wright. 1991. $9.95. Lyons & Burford.

*Streamer-Fly Fishing*, John Merwin. 1991. $9.95. Lyons & Burford.

*Terrestrials: A Modern Approach to Fishing & Tying with Synthetic & Natural Materials*, Harrison R. Steeves III and Ed Koch. 1994. $29.95. Stackpole Books.

## BASS AND PANFISH
*Bassin' with a Fly Rod: One Fly Rodder's Approach to Serious Bass Fishing*, Jack Ellis. 1995. $22.95. Lyons & Burford.

*Bass Flies*, Dick Stewart. 1990. $12.95. Mountain Pond Publishers.

*Fly Rodding for Bass*, Charles F. Waterman. 1989. $9.95. Lyons & Burford.

*The Sunfishes*, Jack Ellis. 1995. $12.95. Lyons & Burford.

## FUN READING
*The Compleat Angler*, or, *The Contemplative Man's Recreation: Being a Discourse of Rivers, Fishponds, Fish and Fishing Not Unworthy of the Perusal of Most Anglers*, Izaak Walton. 1995. $23.00. Ecco Press.

*The Complete Fly Fisherman: the Notes and Letters of Theodore Gordon*, Theodore Gordon. Not in print but available in libraries.

*The Habit of Rivers: Reflections on Trout Streams & Fly Fishing*, Ted Leeson. 1995. $10.95. Lyons & Burford.

*A River Runs Through It: And Other Stories*, Norman Maclean. Several editions in print.

*Spring Creek*, Nick Lyons. 1992. $20.00. Grove Atlantic.

*Treatise on Fishing with a Hook*, Juliana Berners. Not in print but available in libraries.

*Where the Trout are All as Long as Your Leg*, John Gierach. 1993. $9.00. Fireside.

*Whitefish Can't Jump, Other Tales of Gamefish on the Fly*, E. Donnall Thomas, Jr. 1994. $19.95 Ragged Mountain Press.

# VIDEOS
You can learn a great deal from a good video. At the very least you may be inspired by watching a pro go through his or her paces.

*Trailside:® Make Your Own Adventure®*
Our video series was originally broadcast on public television. All Trailside® videos may be purchased by calling 800-872-4574. A catalog is available.

*Fly Fishing in Wyoming*. Fishing for brook trout in the Wind River Range; discussions of tackle, choosing flies and reading water. 40 minutes, $19.98.

A selection of other videos presenting invaluable instruction in fly casting and fly tying include:

## FLY CASTING
*Essence of Fly Casting*. Basics and more with Mel Kreiger. 60 minutes, $29.95.

*Fly Fishing for Striped Bass*. With Jeff Mancini. 83 minutes, $29.95.

*Learning to Fly Fish for Trout*. Basics and equipment with Jack Dennis. 90 minutes, $19.95.

*Lee Wulff on the Beaverkill*. Michael Gold. 85 minutes, $24.95.

*Nymphing*. Complete nymph fishing techniques with Gary Borger. 30 minutes, $29.95.

## FLIES AND FLY TYING
*The Art of Tying the Nymph*. A companion to the book by Skip Morris. 60 minutes, $26.95.

*Fly Tying Made Clear and Simple*. Tools, materials, hooks and tips with Skip Morris. 120 minutes, $26.95.

*Tying and Fishing Attractors*. Dry fishing on the Green River, with Gary LaFontaine. 90 minutes, $19.95.

*Tying and Fishing Caddisflies*. How to tie expert caddisflies and fish with them, with Gary LaFontaine. 120 minutes, $19.95.

*Tying & Fishing Saltwater Flies* (I, II). With Jimmy Nix. 120 minutes each, $19.95 each.

## MAIL-ORDER SOURCES OF BOOKS & VIDEOS

Here are a few mail-order suppliers of both fly-fishing books and videos to get you started.

### ADVENTUROUS TRAVELER BOOKSTORE
P.O. Box 577
Hinesburg, VT 05461
800-282-3963 or 802-482-3330;
fax 800-282-3963 or
802-482-3546
E-mail: *books@atbook.com*
Home page: *http://www.gorp.com/atbook.htm*

### ANGLER'S ART
Barry Serviente
Box 148
Plainfield, PA 17081
717-243-9721; 800-848-1020

### ANGLER'S BOOK SUPPLY
1380 West Second Avenue
Eugene, OR 97402
800-260-3869

### BACKCOUNTRY BOOKSTORE
P.O. Box 6235
Lynnwood, WA 90836-0235
206-290-7652

### TRAILSIDE DIRECT
P.O. Box 5024
Bristol, CT 06011-5024
1 800 TRAILSIDE;
(1-800-872-4574

### WILDERNESS ADVENTURES
Box 1410
Bozeman, MT 59771
406-763-4900

## MAIL-ORDER SOURCES OF EQUIPMENT

There are many of these, from giants like L. L. Bean, Cabela's, and Orvis down to small mom-and-pop fly shops around the country that supplement their walk-in trade with small catalogs. A few of the major mail-order houses are listed here, but don't let that stop you from experimenting with smaller ones when you encounter their ads in the fly-fishing magazines.

### AMERICAN ANGLING SUPPLIES
23 Main Street
Salem, NH 03079
603-893-3333

### CABELA'S
812-13th Avenue
Sidney, NE 69160
800-255-2395; 800-237-4444
Ask for spring fishing/fly-fishing catalog.

### DAN BAILEY'S FLY SHOP
Box 1019-B
Livingston, MT 59047
406-222-1673

### FEATHER-CRAFT
8307 Manchester Road
Box 19904
Street Louis, MO 63144
800-659-1707

### FISHING CREEK OUTFITTERS
Box 301-1
Benton, PA 17814
717-925-2225

### THE FLY SHOP
4140 Churn Creek Road
Reading, CA 96002
916-222-3555

### HUNTER'S ANGLING SUPPLIES
Box 300
New Boston, NH 03070
603-487-3388

### KAUFMANN'S STREAMBORN
Box 23032
Portland, Or 97281
800-442-4359

### L.L. BEAN
Freeport, ME 04033
800-221-4221
Ask for annual fly-fishing catalog.

### MARRIOTT'S FLY-FISHING STORE
2700 West Orangethorpe
Fullerton, CA 92633
714-525-1827

### ORVIS
Manchester, VT 05254
800-541-3541
Ask for spring fishing catalog.

### URBAN ANGLER, LTD.
118 East 25th Street
New York, NY 10010
800-255-5488

## MANUFACTURERS OF EQUIPMENT

Most major fly-tackle makers offer colorful catalogs designed to offer general fly-fishing information as well as details about the products themselves. Still more catalogs for which you can write!

### AARON REELS
10141 Suite 9 Evening Star Drive
Grass Valley, CA 95945
*reels*

### ABEL AUTOMATICS, INC.
165 Aviador Street
Camarillo, CA 93010
805-484-8789; fax 805-482-0701
*reels*

### ADAMS REELS
91 Fairfax Street
West Haven, CT 06516
*reels*

### ASCENT REELS
2516 Fulton Street
Berkeley, CA 94704
*reels*

### BERKLEY
One Berkley Drive
Spirit Lake, IA 51360-1041
712-336-1520
*full line*

### CORTLAND LINE COMPANY
3736 Kellog Road
Box 5588
Cortland, NY 13045
607-756-2851
*fly lines; full line*

### EAGLE CLAW FISHING TACKLE
P.O. Box 16011
Denver, CO 80216
303-321-1481; fax 303-321-4750
*rods, reels, and hooks*

**FENWICK**
5242 Argosy Avenue
Huntington Beach, CA 92649
714-897-1066
*rods, reels*

**GRAPHITE-USA**
7569 Convoy Court
San Diego, CA 92111
619-560-4872
*rods*

**ISLANDER REELS**
6771 Kirkpatrick Crescent
Saanichton, B. C.
Canada V8M 1Z8
604-544-1440
*reels*

**L. L. BEAN**
Freeport, ME 04033
800-221-4221
*full line*

**G. LOOMIS, INC.**
1359 Down River Drive
Woodland, WA 98674
360-225-6516; fax 360-225-7169
*rods and reels*

**THE ORVIS COMPANY**
Manchester, VT 05254
800-235-9763; fax 540-343-7053
in Canada: 800-541-3541
*full line*

**PEERLESS REEL CO.**
427-3 Amherst Street, Suite 177
Nashua, NH 03063
*reels*

**PENN FISHING TACKLE MGF. CO.**
3028 W. Hunting Park Avenue
Philadelphia, PA 19132-1121
215-229-9415
*rods and reels*

**REDINGTON**
3585 SE Street, Lucie Boulevard
Stuart, FL 34997
800-253-2538; fax 407-220-9957
*rods and reels*

**ROSS REELS**
1 Ponderosa Court
Montrose, CO 81401
970-249-1212; fax 970-249-1834
*reels*

**ROYAL WULFF PRODUCTS**
HCR 1, Box 70
Lew Beach, NY 12758
914-439-4060
*fly lines*

**ST. CROIX ROD CO.**
P.O. Box 279
Park Falls, WI 54552
715-762-3226, 800-826-7042; fax
715-762-3293
*rods*

**SCIENTIFIC ANGLERS**
Building 224-2S-27
3M Center
St. Paul, MN 55144
612-733-9549; fax 612-736-7479
*reels and fly lines*

**STH REELS USA, INC.**
Box 500816
Marathon, FL 33050
800-232-1359
*reels*

**SAGE**
7869 Northeast Day Road
Bainbridge Island, WA 98110
206-842-6608; fax 206-842-6830
*rods and reels*

**SCOTT FLY ROD CO.**
P.O. Box 889, 200 San Miguel
River Drive
Telluride, CO 81435
800-728-7208, 970-728-4191; fax
970-728-5031
*rods*

**SOUTH BEND SPORTING GOODS**
Crystal River & Kensington
1950 Stanley Street
Northbrook, IL 60065
800-622-9662; fax 708-564-2042
*full line*

**TEENY NYMPH COMPANY**
Box 989
Gresham, OR 97030
503-667-6602
*fly lines*

**THOMAS & THOMAS
RODMAKERS, INC.**
P.O. Box 32, 2 Avenue A
Turners Falls, MA 01376
413-863-9727; fax 413-863-9692
*rods; full line*

**TYCOON FIN-NOR**
2021 SW 31st Avenue
Hallandale, FL 33009
305-966-5507
*reels*

**VALENTINE FLY REELS**
Box 95
Chartley, MA 02712
*reels*

**R. L. WINSTON ROD COMPANY**
500 South Main Street, Drawer T
Twin Bridges, MT 59754
406-684-5674; fax 406-684-5533
*rods*

# PHOTO CREDITS

**AMERICAN MUSEUM OF FLY FISHING:** 23, 25, 26, 28, 31

**R. VALENTINE ATKINSON:** 13, 59, 68, 71, 109 (top)

**BARRY & CATHY BECK:** 19, 40 (top), 64, 73, 76, 102, 108, 117, 122, 124, 125, 129, 130, 131, 132, 138, 139, 152, 153, 154, 158, 159, 160 (top), 162, 163

**ROB BOSSI/COURTESY L.L. BEAN:** 18, 50 (top left, bottom), 51, 62, 63, 74

**JOHN GOODMAN:** 34 (all), 48 (both), 49 (bottom), 50 (top right), 99, 109 (both bottom), 110 (both), 111 (top), 112 (right), 115, 119 (both), 121 (all), 127, 137, 147 (both), 148 (both), 151, 155 (bottom), 157, 160 (bottom), 165, 167, 175, 176 (all, bottom), 177 (all), 178 (all), 179 (all), 180 (all)

**ED JAWOROWSKI:** 116, 123, 133, 134, 140, 146, 150

**COURTESY L.L. BEAN:** 11, 33, 35, 38, 39, 40 (bottom), 41, 42 (bottom), 45, 46 (all), 47 (all), 49 (top), 52 (both), 53, 56, 58, 69, 70 (both), 72 (all), 77 (both), 161, 168

**BECKY LUIGART-STAYNER:** 55 (both)

**BRIAN O'KEEFE:** 8, 12, 13, 16, 20, 54, 66, 75, 101, 103, 106, 107, 111 (bottom), 112 (left), 114, 118, 120, 126, 128, 155 (top), 156, 176 (top)

**SAM TALARICO:** 17, 21, 37, 42 (top), 142, 143, 144, 149

# INDEX